# 15 Selected Units of English through the News Media

## ―2023 Edition―

Masami Takahashi

Noriko Itoh

Richard Powell

Asahi Press

記事提供
The New York Times
New York Post
The Japan Times
The Guardian
Forbes
AFP-JIJI

写真提供
アフロ：The New York Times／Redux／
ロイター／AP／WESTEND61
AFP／WAA

地図・イラスト
ヨシオカユリ

*15 Selected Units of English through the News Media —2023 Edition—*

# は し が き

　本書は、世界のニュースを通して Reading, Listening, Speaking, Writing のバランスのとれた学習が効果的にできるように工夫してあります。2021年10月：人類と気候変動との関わりに対する研究でノーベル物理学賞、11月：大谷翔平選手　ア・リーグMVPに誰もが納得；仕事の未来：流行りの職場５選、12月：スリランカ　有機農法を始めて大惨事に、2022年１月：アフリカでクーデター多発の理由、２月：気候変動は人類の順応より早く地球をダメにする、３月：韓国での「多文化主義」とは；ビゴレクシア（筋肉醜形恐怖症）とは；アブラモヴィッチの資産凍結でチェルシーが危機状態に；民族主義と帝国主義に基づくプーチンのウクライナ戦争；中国　離婚率と結婚率低下、４月：ベンガル湾で大洪水　住民はマングローブの森に避難；シンガポール　「不当感」の増大で死刑反対意見強まる；リオのカーニバルのパレードを巡り争い騒ぎ；トルコで超インフレとの戦い；ロシア人　プーチン政権から逃れ、ウクライナ避難民と共にイスラエルに；大谷翔平選手　「神懸かりな」歴史的夜、まで世界中のニュースを満載しております。

　The New York Times, The Japan Times, The Guardian, New York Post, Forbes から社会・文化・政治経済・情報・言語・教育・科学・医学・環境・娯楽・スポーツなどのあらゆる分野を網羅しましたので、身近に世界中のニュースに触れ、読み、聞き、話し、書く楽しさを育みながら、多角的にそして複眼的に英語運用力が自然に培われるように意図しています。

　15課より構成され、各課に新聞記事読解前にBefore you readを設けました。本文の内容が予想できる写真と、どこにあるかを示す地図と国の情報を参照しながら自由に意見交換をします。次の Words and Phrases では、記事に記載されている単語や熟語とそれに合致する英語の説明を選び、あらかじめ大事な語の理解を深めて行きます。Summaryでは記事の内容を予想しながら、５語を適当な箇所に記入して要約文を完成させます。記事読解前では難しいようであれば、読解後に活用しても良いと思います。さらに、記事に関連した裏話も載せました。記事の読解にあたり、わかり易い註釈を記事の右端に付け、理解度をチェックするための Multiple Choice, True or False, 記事に関連した語法を学ぶVocabularyと豊富に取り揃えました。Summaryと記事がそのまま音声化されたファイルをウェブ上にあげています。多方面に渡る記事やExercisesを活用して、英字新聞に慣れ親しみ、使っていただけることを望んでいます。

　今回テキスト作成に際して、お世話になりました朝日出版社社長原雅久氏、編集部の日比野忠氏、小川洋一郎氏に心からお礼申し上げます。


2022年10月

高橋　優身

伊藤　典子

Richard Powell

# CONTENTS

# 15 Selected Units of English through the News Media 2023 Edition

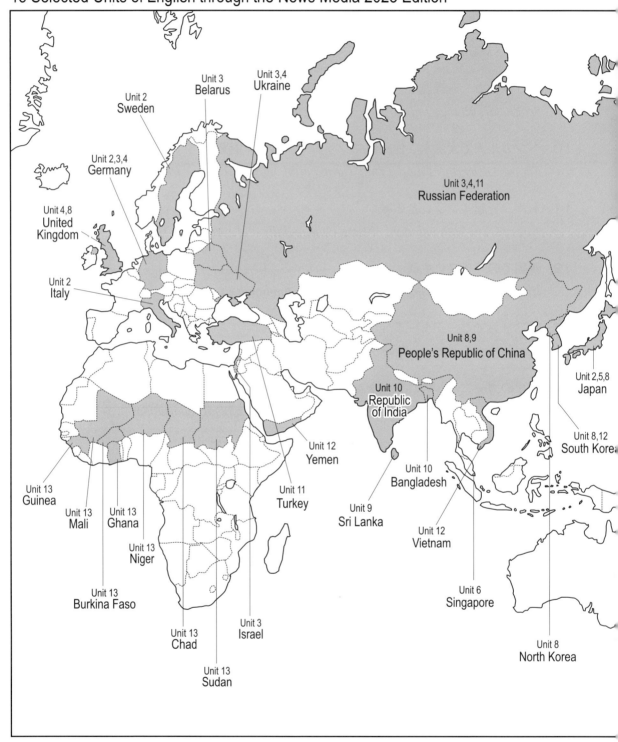

Unit 2
Sweden

Unit 3
Belarus

Unit 3,4
Ukraine

Unit 2,3,4
Germany

Unit 3,4,11
Russian Federation

Unit 4,8
United
Kingdom

Unit 2
Italy

Unit 8,9
People's Republic of China

Unit 2,5,8
Japan

Unit 10
Republic
of India

Unit 8,12
South Korea

Unit 12
Yemen

Unit 11
Turkey

Unit 10
Bangladesh

Unit 13
Guinea

Unit 9
Sri Lanka

Unit 13
Mali

Unit 13
Ghana

Unit 12
Vietnam

Unit 13
Niger

Unit 6
Singapore

Unit 13
Burkina Faso

Unit 13
Chad

Unit 3
Israel

Unit 8
North Korea

Unit 13
Sudan

Unit 5,13
Canada

Unit 1,2,3,5,9,15
U.S.A.

Unit 14
Brazil

## 音声再生アプリ「リスニング・トレーナー」を使った音声ダウンロード

朝日出版社開発のアプリ、「リスニング・トレーナー（リストレ）」を使えば、教科書の音声をスマホ、タブレットに簡単にダウンロードできます。どうぞご活用ください。

### ◉ アプリ【リスニング・トレーナー】の使い方

《アプリのダウンロード》

App Store または Google Play から「リスニング・トレーナー」のアプリ（無料）をダウンロード

App Storeはこちら▶

Google Playはこちら▶

《アプリの使い方》

① アプリを開き「コンテンツを追加」をタップ
② 画面上部に【15697】を入力し Done をタップ

## 音声ストリーミング配信 》》》

この教科書の音声は、右記ウェブサイトにて無料で配信しています。

https://text.asahipress.com/free/english/

# 15 Selected Units of
# English through the News Media

# ●気候変動は人類の順応より早く地球をダメにする

フィリピン・マニラ首都圏の低地に沿う護岸。これで高潮から住民を守れるのか？大丈夫？

The New York Times ／ Redux ／アフロ

## *Before you read*

### Questions

**1.** What do you think the article will be about?

この記事は何の話題についてだと思いますか？

**2.** Do you think it is already too late to stop global warming?

地球温暖化を止めるにはもう手遅れだと思いますか？

## Words and Phrases

次の1〜5の語の説明として最も近いものをa〜eから1つ選び、（　）内に記入しなさい。

| | | | | |
|---|---|---|---|---|
| **1.** convene | （　） | | **a.** | shortage |
| **2.** unleash | （　） | | **b.** | release something dangerous |
| **3.** damning | （　） | | **c.** | impossible to heal or restore |
| **4.** scarcity | （　） | | **d.** | assemble for a meeting |
| **5.** irreversible | （　） | | **e.** | blameworthy |

## Summary

次の英文は記事の要約です。下の語群から最も適切な語を1つ選び、（　）内に記入しなさい。

A new report commissioned by the U.N. (　　　) that we are not taking global warming seriously. More and more people are being (　　　) by floods, droughts, extreme heat or crop failures. Although some countries have taken temporary (　　　) they are not nearly enough. (　　　) we cut fossil fuel consumption global warming will (　　　) get worse.

affected　　concludes　　measures　　only　　unless

　　国連の気候変動に関する政府間パネル（IPCC）による第6次評価報告書が、2021年8月から2022年4月にかけて順次公表された。22年4月現在、気温はすでに1.1度上昇しているが、1.5度以下に抑えるという目標のため、2025年までに二酸化炭素（$CO_2$）などの温室効果ガス排出量を減少させ、$CO_2$の回収や貯蔵を進める必要があると訴えている。対策として、発電分野では化石燃料から温室効果ガスを出さない再生可能エネルギーへの転換をはかり、電気自動車（EV）の導入、建物の断熱化やテレワークを進める。

　　また、再生エネルギーの太陽光発電とリチウムイオン電池は85%、風力発電は55%のコスト削減があり導入し易くなった。日本は、温室効果ガス排出量について「2030年度に46%減」「50年に実質ゼロ」の目標を掲げている。気候市民会議の取り組みが欧州で始められて以来、日本でも色々な立場の市民の意見を反映させ、地球温暖化問題を「自分事」として捉えてもらおうと取り組みが行われている。

　　ところが、2022年2月ロシアのウクライナ侵攻で、世界のエネルギー事情は一変した。ロシアに経済制裁を課しているため、ロシアからのエネルギーに依存していた欧州各国は、温室効果ガスを出す石炭火力など、使えるものは何でも使っている。原油価格や天然ガス価格が最高値を示している。日本はエネルギー自給率が11%しかなく、ロシアへの経済制裁前は、天然ガスの9%、石油の4%をロシアから輸入していた。気候変動対策とエネルギー安全保障を両立させるためには、再生可能エネルギーの利用拡大、省エネの推進、原子力発電の活用を考えなければならない。

03

# Climate Change Is Harming the Planet Faster Than We Can Adapt, U.N. Warns

Countries aren't doing nearly enough to protect against the disasters to come as the planet keeps heating up, a major new scientific report concludes.

The dangers of climate change are mounting so rapidly
5 that they could soon overwhelm the ability of both nature and humanity to adapt unless greenhouse gas emissions are quickly reduced, according to a major new scientific report released on Monday.

04

The report by the Intergovernmental Panel on Climate
10 Change, a body of experts convened by the United Nations, is the most detailed look yet at the threats posed by global warming. It concludes that nations aren't doing nearly enough to protect cities, farms and coastlines from the hazards that climate change has unleashed so far, such as record droughts
15 and rising seas, let alone from the even greater disasters in store as the planet continues to warm.

Written by 270 researchers from 67 countries, the report is "an atlas of human suffering and a damning indictment of failed climate leadership," said António Guterres, the United
20 Nations secretary general.

05

In 2019, storms, floods and other extreme weather events displaced more than 13 million people across Asia and Africa. Rising heat and drought are killing crops and trees, putting millions worldwide at increased risk of hunger and
25 malnutrition, while mosquitoes carrying diseases like malaria and dengue are spreading into new areas. Roughly half the world's population currently faces severe water scarcity at least part of the year.

To date, many nations have been able to partly limit
30 the damage by spending billions of dollars each year on adaptation measures like flood barriers, air-conditioning or

| | |
|---|---|
| to come：来たるべき《未来を示し、直前の名詞を修飾》 | |
| overwhelm ～：～を圧倒する | |
| greenhouse gas emission：温室効果ガス排出 | |
| reduced：削減される | |
| body：集まり | |
| convened：召集された | |
| look at ～：～についての考察 | |
| posed：もたらされた | |
| let alone ～：～はもちろん、言うまでもなく | |
| in store：差し迫る | |
| indictment of ～：～に対する起訴 | |
| failed climate leadership：気候変動に関してリーダーシップが発揮できなかったこと | |
| secretary general：事務総長 | |
| extreme weather events：異常気象 | |
| malnutrition：栄養失調 | |
| dengue：デング熱 | |
| water scarcity：水不足 | |
| To date：今日まで | |
| flood barriers：防潮堤 | |

early-warning systems for tropical cyclones.

But those efforts are too often "incremental," the report said. Preparing for future threats, like dwindling freshwater supplies or irreversible ecosystem damage, will require "transformational" changes that involve rethinking how people build homes, grow food, produce energy and protect nature.

The report also carries a stark warning: If temperatures keep rising, many parts of the world could soon face limits in how much they can adapt to a changing environment. If nations don't act quickly to slash fossil fuel emissions and halt global warming, more and more people will suffer unavoidable loss or be forced to flee their homes, creating dislocation on a global scale.

If average warming passes 1.5 degrees Celsius, even humanity's best efforts to adapt could falter, the report warns. The cost of defending coastal communities against rising seas could exceed what many nations can afford. In some regions, including parts of North America, livestock and outdoor workers could face rising levels of heat stress that make farming increasingly difficult, said Rachel Bezner Kerr, an agricultural expert at Cornell University who contributed to the report.

Poor nations are far more exposed to climate risks than rich countries. Between 2010 and 2020, droughts, floods and storms killed 15 times as many people in highly vulnerable countries, including those in Africa and Asia, as in the wealthiest countries, the report said.

by Brad Plummer and Raymond Zhong
*The New York Times, February 28, 2022*

tropical cyclones：熱帯低気圧

"incremental"：「漸進的な」

dwindling：減少する

irreversible：不可逆的な

"transformational"：「変革的な」

stark：厳しい

slash 〜：〜を削減する

fossil fuel：化石燃料

dislocation：混乱

Celsius：摂氏

falter：衰える、弱体化する

15 times：15倍

vulnerable：脆弱な

# Exercises

次の１～５の英文を完成させるために、ａ～ｄの中から最も適切なものを１つ選びなさい。

1. The writer warns that rising greenhouse gas emissions may
   - **a.** harm consumer protection.
   - **b.** bring worldwide crises.
   - **c.** increase the cutting of trees.
   - **d.** see the beginning of global warming.

2. _____ unless the earth can be cooled.
   - **a.** Overwhelming disasters such as floods will strike
   - **b.** More air disasters such as plane crashes will be reported
   - **c.** Terrible disasters such as earthquakes will happen
   - **d.** Financial disasters such as bankruptcies will result

3. Many wealthy nations have been able to restrict the damage by
   - **a.** voting out unpopular governments.
   - **b.** giving help to wealthier citizens.
   - **c.** spending a huge amount of money on flood protection.
   - **d.** increasing the supply of electricity.

4. Rising temperatures and droughts are
   - **a.** halting global emissions.
   - **b.** harming food production.
   - **c.** heating fossil fuels.
   - **d.** humbling politicians.

5. According to the report, measures to deal with the crisis have been
   - **a.** non-existent.
   - **b.** limited and inadequate.
   - **c.** overly ambitious.
   - **d.** irreversible.

## True or False

本文の内容に合致するものにＴ（True）、合致しないものにＦ（False）をつけなさい。

(     ) **1.** If rising heat kills trees and crops, millions of people will get malnourished.

(     ) **2.** One crucial goal is to keep temperature rises under 1.5 degrees.

(     ) **3.** "Transformational" change means rethinking how to produce energy and protect nature.

(     ) **4.** Rich countries suffer fewer climate risks than poor countries.

(     ) **5.** Due to global warming, mosquitos are carrying diseases like smallpox and coronavirus.

## Vocabulary

次の１〜８は、「climate change 気候変動」に関する英文です。日本文に合わせて（   ）内に最も適切な語を下の語群から１つ選び、記入しなさい。

1. 気候変動問題は、緊急の注意を向ける必要がある。

   The (       ) issue requires urgent attention.

2. 地球温暖化は、人類の脅威である。

   (       ) is a threat to mankind.

3. 水力発電は、温室効果ガスの排出量が極めて小さい。

   Hydropower emits almost no (       ) gases.

4. 天然ガスは、化石燃料だ。

   Natural gas is a (       ).

5. 我々は、二酸化炭素を削減する必要がある。

   We need to reduce (       ).

6. 干ばつは、食料不足を招いた。

   The (       ) led to an insufficiency of food.

7. 大雨で道路が冠水した。

   Heavy rains have (       ) the road.

8. 50万人以上の子供たちが、いまだに栄養失調に苦しんでいる。

   More than half a million children still suffer from (       ).

| | | | |
|---|---|---|---|
| carbon dioxide | climate change | drought | flooded |
| fossil fuel | global warming | greenhouse | malnutrition |

# ●人類と気候変動との関わりに対する研究で
## ノーベル物理学賞

「人類と気候変動との関わり」で2021年ノーベル物理学賞を受賞した
眞鍋淑郎博士　　　　　　　　　　　　　　　　　　AFP／WAA

## *Before you read*

### Kingdom of Sweden
### スウェーデン王国

面積　450,000km²（日本の約1.2倍）（世界57位）
人口　10,220,000人（世界91位）
公用語　スウェーデン語
首都　ストックホルム
民族　スウェーデン人　85%
　　　フィンランド人　5%
宗教　キリスト教プロテスタント・ルター派　80%
GDP　5,560億ドル（世界23位）
　　　1人当たり GDP　54,356ドル（世界12位）
通貨　スウェーデン・クローネ
政体　立憲君主制
識字率　99%

次の1～5の語句の説明として最も近いものをa～eから1つ選び、(　)内に記入しなさい。

1. pinpoint　　　　(　　)
2. rigorous　　　　(　　)
3. pave the way　　(　　)
4. human-caused　(　　)
5. fluctuation　　　(　　)

a. give precise information about
b. unstable change
c. resulting from the activity of people
d. provide a foundation
e. disciplined and detailed

## Summary

次の英文は記事の要約です。下の語群から最も適切な語を1つ選び、(　)内に記入しなさい。

08

Scientists (　　　　　) in America, Germany and Italy have shared the Nobel Physics Prize. Through their work on different aspects of (　　　　) change we now understand global warming better. Japan-born Syukuro Manabe developed a model to show (　　　　) between greenhouse gases and warming. This helped Klaus Hasselmann study changes in the (　　　　) and Giorgio Parisi explore fluctuations in the earth's (　　　　).

atmosphere　　based　　climate　　links　　oceans

　　2021年度のノーベル物理学賞は、「地球温暖化を予測する地球気候モデルの開発」で眞鍋淑郎プリンストン大学上席研究員とローマ・サピエンツア大学のジョルジョ・パリージ教授、マックス・プランク気象学研究所のクラウス・ハッセルマン教授に贈られた。
　　眞鍋氏は、1958年にアメリカ気象局の研究員として渡米した。1967年に高速コンピュータを使い、大気の運動との関係を定めるモデルを開発し、「$CO_2$が2倍に増えると地上気温が2.36度上昇する」との予測を明らかにした。さらに、1989年には、大気、海洋、陸上の気象が互いに与える影響を組み込んだ本格的な温暖化予測に成功した。
　　眞鍋氏は、地球を循環する大気や海の流れを物理法則に基づいて定式化し、数値で予測することを考えた。2002年から5期連続で世界最高の計算速度を達成した国産スーパーコンピュータ「地球シュミレーター」を駆使して、地球規模で降水量の分布や海流の状況などを詳しく把握できるようになった。眞鍋氏は、1931年生まれの90歳だが、「外に出て気候がどうなっているかを肌で感じること。何にでも好奇心を持つことが肝心だ」と力を込めて語っていた。

# Reading

09

## Nobel Prize in Physics Awarded for Study of Humanity's Role in Changing Climate

Three scientists received the Nobel Prize in Physics on Tuesday for work that is essential to understanding how the Earth's climate is changing, pinpointing the effect of human behavior on those changes and ultimately predicting the impact of global warming.

The winners were Syukuro Manabe of Princeton University, Klaus Hasselmann of the Max Planck Institute for Meteorology in Hamburg, Germany, and Giorgio Parisi of the Sapienza University of Rome.

10

"The discoveries being recognized this year demonstrate that our knowledge about the climate rests on a solid scientific foundation, based on a rigorous analysis of observations," said Thors Hans Hansson, chair of the Nobel Committee for Physics.

Complex physical systems, such as the climate, are often defined by their disorder. This year's winners helped bring understanding to what seemed like chaos by describing those systems and predicting their long-term behavior.

In 1967, Dr. Manabe developed a computer model that confirmed the critical connection between the primary greenhouse gas — carbon dioxide — and warming in the atmosphere.

That model paved the way for others of increasing sophistication. Dr. Manabe's later models, which explored connections between conditions in the ocean and atmosphere, were crucial to recognizing how increased melting of the Greenland ice sheet could affect ocean circulation in the North Atlantic, said Michael Mann, a climate scientist at Pennsylvania State University.

"He has contributed fundamentally to our understanding of human-caused climate change and dynamical mechanisms," Dr. Mann said.

About a decade after Dr. Manabe's foundational work,

---

Awarded:《大見出しの場合、受動態の be 動詞を省略する》

work:業績

pinpointing 〜:〜を特定する

predicting 〜:〜を予想する

Syukuro Manabe:眞鍋淑郎

Institute for Meteorology:気象学研究所

recognized:表彰される

rests on 〜:〜に基づく

observations:観測

disorder:無秩序

confirmed 〜:〜を確認した

atmosphere:大気

sophistication:洗練さ

ocean:大洋

crucial to 〜:〜にとって重要だ

ocean circulation:海洋循環

dynamical mechanisms:動的メカニズム

12

Dr. Hasselmann created a model that connected short-term climate phenomena — in other words, rain and other kinds of weather — to longer-term climate like ocean and atmospheric currents. Dr. Mann said that work laid the basis for attribution studies, a field of scientific inquiry that seeks to establish the influence of climate change on specific events like droughts, heat waves and intense rainstorms.

Dr. Parisi is credited with the discovery of the interplay of disorder and fluctuations in physical systems, including everything from a tiny collection of atoms to the atmosphere of an entire planet.

All three scientists have been working to understand the complex natural systems that have been driving climate change for decades, and their discoveries have provided the scaffolding on which predictions about climate are built.

The importance of their work has only gained urgency as the forecast models reveal an increasingly dire outlook if the rise in global temperature is not arrested.

Dr. Manabe is a senior meteorologist and climatologist at Princeton University. Born in 1931 in Shingu, Japan, he earned his Ph.D. in 1957 from the University of Tokyo before joining the U.S. Weather Bureau.

Dr. Hasselmann is a German physicist and oceanographer who greatly advanced public understanding of climate change through the creation of a model that links climate and chaotic weather systems. He is a professor at the Max Planck Institute for Meteorology in Hamburg.

Dr. Parisi is an Italian theoretical physicist who was born in 1948 in Rome and whose research has focused on quantum field theory and complex systems.

By Cade Metz, Marc Santora and Cora Engelbrecht
*The New York Times, October 7, 2021*

---

phenomena：現象

laid the basis for 〜：〜の基礎を築いた

inquiry：研究

is credited with 〜：〜で有名

interplay：相互作用

fluctuations：揺らぎ、変動

collection of 〜：〜の集まり

driving 〜：〜を推進してきた

scaffolding：足場

gained urgency：緊急性を増した

forecast：予想

outlook：見通し

arrested：阻止される

Shingu：和歌山県新宮市

Ph.D.：博士号

U.S. Weather Bureau：米国気象局

oceanographer：海洋学者

quantum field theory：「場の量子論」

complex systems：「複雑系」

# Exercises

次の１～５の英文を完成させるために、ａ～ｄの中から最も適切なものを１つ選びなさい。

1. In 2021, three scientists received the Nobel Prize in Physics for their studies that laid the foundation of our knowledge of the Earth's

    **a.** weather and how humanity studies it.
    **b.** climate and how humanity influences it.
    **c.** climate and how science affects it.
    **d.** weather and how science develops it.

2. In 1967, Syukuro Manabe led the development of a computer model

    **a.** proving the link between carbon dioxide and atmospheric warming.
    **b.** providing for the Earth's formation.
    **c.** confirming the connection between information and practice.
    **d.** maintaining data on economic growth.

3. Syukuro Manabe examined links between _____ conditions.

    **a.** greenhouse gas and fossil fuel gas
    **b.** global and local
    **c.** oceanic and atmospheric
    **d.** human and mechanical

4. Hasselmann's work differed from Manabe's by

    **a.** denying climate change.
    **b.** using scientific modelling.
    **c.** analyzing ocean data.
    **d.** linking short-term to long-term phenomena.

5. Giorgio Parisi linked planetary behavior to

    **a.** disorder among scientists.
    **b.** the stable nature of physics.
    **c.** oceanography.
    **d.** the interplay of atoms.

本文の内容に合致するものにＴ（True）、合致しないものにＦ（False）をつけなさい。

( 　 ) **1.** Dr. Manabe is a senior weather forecaster.

( 　 ) **2.** Dr. Hasselmann is a German oceanographer.

( 　 ) **3.** Dr. Parisi is older than Dr. Manabe.

( 　 ) **4.** Dr. Manabe's work laid the foundation for the development of current climate models.

( 　 ) **5.** The winners' main work was done in Japan, Germany and Italy respectively.

## Vocabulary

次の英文は、Nobel Prize Organisation のホームページに掲載された Nobel Prize in Physics『ノーベル賞物理学』の記事の一部です。下の語群から最も適切な語を１つ選び、( 　 ) 内に記入しなさい。

One complex system of vital importance to humankind is Earth's ( 　 ). Syukuro Manabe demonstrated how increased levels of ( 　 ) dioxide in the atmosphere lead to ( 　 ) temperatures at the surface of the Earth. In the 1960s, he led the development of physical models of the Earth's climate and was the first person to explore the interaction between radiation balance and the vertical transport of air masses. His work laid the foundation for the development of current climate models.

About ten years later, Klaus Hasselmann created a model that links ( 　 ) weather and climate, thus answering the question of why climate models can be reliable despite weather being ( 　 ) and chaotic. Around 1980, Giorgio Parisi discovered hidden patterns in disordered complex ( 　 ). His discoveries are among the most important contributions to the theory of complex systems.

"The discoveries being recognised this year demonstrate that our knowledge about the climate rests on a solid scientific foundation, based on a rigorous ( 　 ) of observations. This year's Laureates have all contributed to us gaining deeper insight into the ( 　 ) and evolution of complex physical systems," says Thors Hans Hansson, chair of the Nobel Committee for Physics.

| | | | |
|---|---|---|---|
| analysis | carbon | changeable | climate |
| increased | materials | properties | together |

- ●民族主義と帝国主義に基づくプーチンのウクライナ戦争
- ●ロシア人　プーチン政権から逃れ、ウクライナ避難民と共にイスラエルに

2022年3月11日、クリミアのあるバス停前の広告。プーチン大統領は「ロシアは戦争を始めない、戦争を終わらす」と強調　　　ロイター／アフロ

## *Before you read*

### Russian Federation
### ロシア連邦

面積　17,098,246km²（日本の約45倍）（世界1位）
首都・最大都市　モスクワ
公用語　ロシア語／識字率　99.7%
人口　145,872,000人　（世界9位）
民族　スラブ人　82.7%／テュルク系　8.7%
　　　コーカサス系　3.7%／ウラル系　1.6%
宗教　ロシア正教会　63%／その他のキリスト教　4.5%
　　　イスラム教　6.6%／仏教　0.5%／ユダヤ教　0.6%
GDP　1兆6,572億米ドル（世界12位）
　　　1人当たりのGDP：11,289米ドル（世界65位）
通貨　ロシア・ルーブル
政体　共和制・連邦制

### Ukraine　ウクライナ
ソビエト連邦より1991年8月24日独立

面積　603,700km²（日本の約1.6倍）（世界45位）
首都　キーウ
公用語　ウクライナ語／識字率　99.7%
人口　41,590,000人（南部クリミアを除く）
民族　ウクライナ人　77.8%／ロシア人　17.3%
　　　ベラルーシ人0.6%／モルドバ人、クリミア人、
　　　ユダヤ人等
宗教　ウクライナ正教会　76.5%
　　　その他のキリスト教　4.4%／ユダヤ教0.6%
GDP　5,450億300万米ドル
　　　1人当たりのGDP　13,128米ドル
通貨　フリヴニャ／政体　共和制

次の 1 ～ 5 の語句の説明として最も近いものを a ～ e から 1 つ選び、（　）内に記入しなさい。

| | | | | | |
|---|---|---|---|---|---|
| **1.** wage war | ( | ) | **a.** | so-called | |
| **2.** assert | ( | ) | **b.** | make use of | |
| **3.** assumption | ( | ) | **c.** | attack | |
| **4.** alleged | ( | ) | **d.** | claim | |
| **5.** take advantage of | ( | ) | **e.** | pre-existing or general idea | |

**Summary**

次の英文は記事の要約です。下の語群から最も適切な語を 1 つ選び、（　）内に記入しなさい。

14

While his (　　　　　) believe nations should be based on individual rights and responsibilities, Putin emphasizes collectivist (　　　　　). He justified his attack on Ukraine by (　　　　　) it is part of Russia. Many Russians (　　　　　) with him, and some feel they can no longer live in Russia. Fearing for their safety after making a movie (　　　　　) Putin, two filmmakers fled to Israel.

| claiming | criticizing | disagree | nationalism | opponents |
|---|---|---|---|---|

　　ロシアのプーチン大統領は、2022年 2 月20日の北京冬季五輪閉幕の翌21日にウクライナ東部へのロシア軍派兵を命じ、24日に侵攻を開始した。ロシアは、2021年 3 月にウクライナとの国境地帯や、2014年に併合したウクライナ南部クリミアに大規模な軍部隊を集結させた。これは、ウクライナのゼレンスキー大統領のクリミア奪還に向けた国家戦略を採択したことに対するけん制の動きだった。10月下旬にはロシアはウクライナとの国境地帯に大規模な軍隊を再集結させ、増強を続けた。

　　12月中旬に、ロシアは、米国と北大西洋条約機構（NATO）を拡大せず、ロシアの「安全の保証」に関する条約案を提示し、ウクライナを NATO に加盟させないという要求を出した。この要求が拒否されれば「軍事技術的な対応」をとると警告した。バイデン大統領、マクロン大統領、ショルツ首相らも仲介に乗り出したが、不発に終わった。このウクライナ侵攻は、米国が主導する NATO が支えて来たヨーロッパの安全保障体制に、ロシアが武力で公然と挑戦したことになる。

　　ウクライナには、人口の約 2 割、800万人以上のロシア人が居住している。肥沃な農地に恵まれ、軍需・宇宙産業の拠点となっている。ロシアは帝政、ソ連時代にウクライナを支配し、両国は同じスラブ系民族で、ロシアを兄、ウクライナを弟とする「兄弟国家」と呼ばれて来た。しかし、長年に渡るロシアの圧迫は、ウクライナを欧米へと接近させている。米国、EU 諸国、日本などが対ロシア経済制裁を発動しているため、ロシア経済は大打撃を受けているが、制裁を課した国々にも原油やガスのエネルギー価格の急騰で物価上昇が続いている。

15

## Putin's War on Ukraine Is About Ethnicity and Empire

BRUSSELS — President Biden took office with the idea that this century's struggle would be between the world's democracies and autocracies.

But in waging war on Ukraine, President Vladimir V.
5 Putin of Russia has been driven by a different concept, ethno-nationalism. It is an idea of nationhood and identity based on language, culture and blood — a collectivist ideology with deep roots in Russian history and thought.

Mr. Putin has repeatedly asserted that Ukraine is not a real
10 state and that the Ukrainians are not a real people, but actually Russian, part of a Slavic heartland that also includes Belarus.

16

"Putin wants to consolidate the civilizational border of Russia, as he calls it, and he is doing that by invading a sovereign European country," said Ivan Vejvoda, a senior
15 fellow at the Institute of Human Sciences in Vienna.

For Mr. Putin's opponents in Ukraine and the West, nations are built on civic responsibility, the rule of law and the rights of individuals and minorities, including free expression and a free vote.

20 "What Russia is doing is not just making war against an innocent nation here," said Timothy Snyder, a professor at Yale who has written extensively about Russia and Ukraine, but attacking assumptions about a peaceful Europe that respects borders, national sovereignty and multilateral institutions.

By Stephen Erlanger
*The New York Times, March 16, 2022*

25
17

## Russians flee Putin regime to join Ukraine refugees in Israel

AFP Rehovot, Israel — The moment Russian tanks rolled

Ethnicity：民族主義

took office：就任した

autocracies：専制主義、独裁政治

waging war：会戦

ethno-nationalism：民族国家主義

nationhood：国民性

collectivist：集産主義的《土地・生産手段などを国家が管理する》

asserted 〜：〜と主張した

consolidate 〜：〜を強化する

sovereign：独立国の

Institute of Human Sciences：人間科学研究所

Vienna：ウィーン

opponents：反対派

assumptions：仮定

multilateral institutions：多国間機関

regime：政権

refugees：避難民

AFP：AFP-JIJI《記事の配信会社：自社作成の記事ではなく配信会社から入手した記事》

rolled into 〜：〜に侵入した

into Ukraine, Russian filmmakers Anna Shishova-Bogolyubova and Dmitry Bogolyubov knew they had to leave Moscow.

30　"We were the next on the list," the couple said in their borrowed flat in Rehovot, a quiet Israeli city 20 kilometers (12 miles) south of Tel Aviv.

flat：アパート

Once you're on the list of alleged "foreign agents," you face a life of "self-censorship or, sooner or later, prison," 35 said Bogolyubov, who directed the German-financed 2019 documentary "Town of Glory".

alleged ～：～と推定された（人物）

self-censorship：自己検閲

The film portrays President Vladimir Putin's use of references related to the fight against Nazi Germany to establish his authority in Russian villages.

references：言及

40　As its international isolation has deepened, Moscow has come to view all movies made with foreign financing with suspicion, including documentaries, and the couple said theirs was no exception.

isolation：孤立

with suspicion：疑って

"Over the past few years, we felt threatened. In the past 45 few months in particular, people were spying on us and taking photographs on our film sets," Shishova-Bogolyubova said.

The couple decided to continue working in Russia but, taking advantage of their Jewish ancestry, they obtained Israeli citizenship just in case.

taking advantage of ～：～を利用する

just in case：万が一に備えて

50　Since Russian troops invaded on February 24, nearly 24,000 Ukrainians have fled to Israel, some but not all taking advantage of the law, according to immigration ministry figures.

immigration ministry figures：移民省の統計

They have been joined by around 10,000 Russians, said an 55 Israeli immigration official.

official：当局者

The wave of immigration from Ukraine and Russia over the past seven weeks is the largest Israel has seen since the early 1990s when the collapse of the Soviet Union prompted hundreds of thousands to seek a new life on the shores of the 60 Mediterranean.

collapse：崩壊

prompted ～ to …：～に…するよう促した

*The Japan Times, April 17, 2022*

# *Exercises*

## Multiple Choice

次の 1 ～ 5 の英文を完成させるために、a ～ d の中から最も適切なものを 1 つ選びなさい。

1. Putin's invasion of Russia reflects his belief that
    **a.** his own race is more important than others.
    **b.** Russia needs to recruit Ukrainian soldiers.
    **c.** international borders must be respected.
    **d.** nations are based on history rather than political choice.

2. Putin emphasizes
    **a.** similarities among all the people of Europe.
    **b.** similarities between the Ukrainians and Belarussians.
    **c.** differences between the Russians and other Slavic people.
    **d.** differences between freedom of expression and voting rights.

3. According to the article, Putin justified his attack on Ukraine by claiming
    **a.** it is part of Russia.
    **b.** it is next to Russia.
    **c.** it is autocratic.
    **d.** it is democratic.

4. Bogolyubov's documentary "Town of Glory" describes Putin's
    **a.** imprisonment of foreign journalists.
    **b.** patriotic war against Ukraine.
    **c.** exploitation of nostalgia to increase his authority.
    **d.** life as a solider during the Second World War.

5. Since the invasion of Ukraine, Israel has received thousands of refugees
    **a.** who support the ongoing war.
    **b.** from Ukraine but not Russia.
    **c.** who are victims of the collapse of the Soviet Union.
    **d.** from both Russia and Ukraine.

本文の内容に合致するものにT（True）、合致しないものにF（False）をつけなさい。

( ) **1.** With the collapse of the Soviet Union in 1990, many people migrated to Iraq.

( ) **2.** Germany financially supported the film "Town of Glory."

( ) **3.** The makers of "Town of Glory" applied for citizenship upon arrival in Israel.

( ) **4.** Putin believes in ethno-nationalism based on language, culture and blood.

( ) **5.** Putin wants to fortify the Russian border by invading Ukraine and Belarus.

**Vocabulary**

次の英文は、読売新聞の The Japan News「えいご工房」に掲載された *Crisis escalates as migrants attempt to storm into Poland*『ポーランドへ流入試みる移民で危機深刻化』の記事の一部です。下の語群から最も適切な語を1つ選び、（　）内に記入しなさい。

WARSAW (AP) — Hundreds, if not thousands, of migrants sought to (　　　　) the border from Belarus into (　　　　) on Nov. 8, cutting razor wire fences and using branches to try and climb over them. The siege escalated a crisis along the European Union's eastern border that has been (　　　　) for months.

Poland's Defense Ministry posted a video showing an armed Polish officer using a (　　　　) spray through a fence at men who were trying to cut the (　　　　) wire.

A spokesman for Poland's security forces stressed that the "large groups of migrants ... are fully controlled by the Belarusian security services and army." He (　　　　) Belarusian President Alexander Lukashenko of acting to (　　　　) Poland and other EU countries to pressure the bloc into dropping its sanctions on Minsk. Those sanctions were put into place after Belarus (　　　　) down brutally on democracy protests.

| accused | chemical | cracked | destabilize |
|---------|----------|---------|-------------|
| Poland  | razor    | simmering | storm     |

## ●アブラモヴィッチの資産凍結でチェルシーが危機状態に

ロシアのウクライナ侵攻で、名門サッカー・クラブが危機に。チェルシーのホーム・スタジアム入口のロゴマーク　　　　　　　　ロイター／アフロ

## *Before you read*

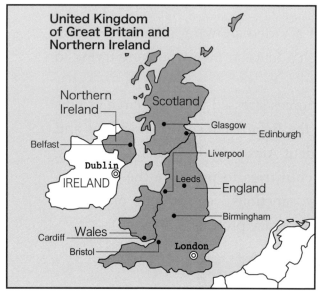

the United Kingdom of Great Britain and Northern Ireland
**英国（グレートブリテン及びアイルランド連合王国）**

面積　244,820km²（日本の本州と四国とほぼ同じ）
　　　（世界78位）
人口　67,530,000人（世界21位）
公用語　英語
首都　ロンドン
民族　イングランド人　5,500万人
　　　スコットランド人　540万人
　　　（北）アイルランド人　181万人
　　　ウエールズ人　300万人
宗教　キリスト教　71.6%／イスラム教徒　2.7%
　　　ヒンドゥ教　1.0%
GDP　2兆8,288億ドル（世界5位）／
　　　1人当たりGDP　42,580ドル（世界22位）
通貨　UKポンド
政体　立憲君主制
識字率　99%

次の1〜5の語句の説明として最も近いものをa〜eから1つ選び、(　)内に記入しなさい。

| | | | | | |
|---|---|---|---|---|---|
| **1.** | text messages | (　) | **a.** | short communications sent by smartphone |
| **2.** | holdings | (　) | **b.** | need to be very careful about money |
| **3.** | untenable | (　) | **c.** | distribute |
| **4.** | austerity | (　) | **d.** | impossible to maintain or defend |
| **5.** | dispense | (　) | **e.** | financial or property assets |

**Summary**

次の英文は記事の要約です。下の語群から最も適切な語を1つ選び、(　)内に記入しなさい。

20

Like many wealthy Russians (　　　　) to Putin, Roman Abramovich has had his assets frozen. This means he can sell (　　　) Chelsea Football Club nor its players or (　　　　). The British government has promised that players and staff will still be (　　　) and fans will still be able to watch matches. But this is a worrying and (　　　) time for the club.

close　　confusing　　merchandise　　neither　　paid

ロマン・アブラモヴィッチは、1966年生まれのユダヤ系ロシア人の実業家である。3歳のときに両親を亡くし、孤児として育った。ソ連崩壊後の1992年26歳のとき、商売を始め、特に石油取引業で巨万の富を得た。34歳で、チュクチ自治管区の知事に選出され、8年間勤めた。ロシアの新興財閥オリガルヒの一人として、政治家や官僚との関係で存在を拡大させていった。知事就任3年後の2003年に、イングランドのサッカー・クラブのチェルシーを買収し、約160億円の負債を返済し、次々と有力選手を獲得し、アブラモヴィッチの名は、世界中に知られるようになった。

2022年2月24日にロシアのウクライナ侵攻が始まり、ウクライナ側の要請により、仲介者としてウクライナとロシアとの和平交渉に関与した。その際、アブラモヴィッチとウクライナ側の代表団の目の充血、顔や手の皮膚の剥がれる症状を訴え、毒物が投与されたとメディアは報道している。彼は、プーチン大統領やユダヤ人勢力との関係を保ちながら西側に根を下ろそうと努力し特異な立場をとって来た。

2022年3月12日にプレミア・リーグ側がアブラモヴィッチを失格処分にした。その後、英国政府は、チェルシーFCの運営継続を許可する特別ライセンスを発行し、アブラモヴィッチが取引から利益を得ない限り、クラブの売却を認める声明を出した。MLBカブスのオーナー、NFLジェッツのオーナー、MLBドジャースのオーナー・ベーリーとスイスの大富豪ヴィスらと組んだコンソーシアム等が買収に興味を示した。2022年5月にチェルシーがベーリーのコンソーシアムに42億5000万ポンド（約6,800億円）で売却され、政府の承認を得た。売却の純収益を慈善事業に寄付し、チェルシーへの貸付けの返済を求めないことを約束した。

21

## Britain Freezes Assets of Roman Abramovich, Creating Crisis at Chelsea

LONDON — For Chelsea F.C.'s players and coaches, the first snippets of information arrived in the text messages and news alerts that pinged their cellphones as they made their way to a private terminal at London's Gatwick Airport on
5 Thursday morning.

The British government had frozen the assets of their team's Russian owner, Roman Abramovich, as part of a wider set of sanctions announced against a group of Russian oligarchs. The action, part of the government's response to
10 Russia's invasion of Ukraine, was designed to punish a handful of individuals whose businesses, wealth and connections are closely associated with the Kremlin. Abramovich, the British government said, has enjoyed a "close relationship" with Russia's president, Vladimir V. Putin, for decades.

22

15 The order applied to all of Abramovich's businesses, properties and holdings, but its most consequential — and most high-profile — effect hit Chelsea, the reigning European soccer champion, which was at that very moment beginning its journey to a Thursday night Premier League match at
20 Norwich City.

News reports and government statements slowly filled in some of the gaps: Abramovich's plans to sell the team were now untenable, and on hold; the club was forbidden from selling tickets or merchandise, lest any of the money feed back
25 to its owner; and the team was prohibited — for the moment — from acquiring or selling players in soccer's multibillion-dollar trading market.

And hour by nervous hour, one more thing became clear: Chelsea, one of Europe's leading teams and a contender for
30 another Champions League title this season, was suddenly facing a worrisome future marked by austerity, uncertainty

Assets：資産

Chelsea：チェルシー《1905年設立のロンドン西部のフラムに本拠を置くプロサッカー・クラブ》

alerts：通知《名詞》

pinged 〜：〜にピーンという音を出させた

made their way to 〜：〜に向かっていた

sanctions against 〜：〜に対する制裁措置

oligarchs：オリガルヒ、新興財閥

properties：財産

holdings：持ち株

high-profile：注目を集める

Premier League：プレミア・リーグ

untenable：受け入れ難い

on hold：保留状態

lest 〜：〜しないように

for the moment：今のところ

contender：候補

austerity：緊縮財政

and decay.

Even as it announced its actions against Abramovich and six other Russian oligarchs, the government said it had
35 taken steps to ensure Chelsea would be able to continue its operations and complete its season. To protect the club's interests, the government said, it had issued Chelsea a license allowing it to continue its soccer-related activities.

The license, which the government said would be under
40 "constant review," will ensure that the team's players and staff will continue to be paid; that fans holding season tickets can continue to attend games; and that the integrity of the Premier League, which is considered an important cultural asset and one of Britain's most high-profile exports, will not be affected.

45 But the sanctions will put a stranglehold on Chelsea's spending and seriously undermine its ability to operate at the levels it has for the past two decades.

An uncertain future awaits, with the sanctions affecting everything from the money Chelsea spends on travel to how
50 it dispenses the tens of millions of dollars it receives from television broadcasters.

At the club on Thursday morning, staff members were struggling to come to terms with what the government's actions would mean for them, their jobs and the team. Many
55 club officials, including Chelsea's coach, Thomas Tuchel, a German, and Abramovich's chief lieutenant, the club director Marina Granovskaia, were still trying to understand what they could and could not do.

By Tariq Panja
*The New York Times, March 10, 2022*

decay：衰退

taken steps：措置を講じた
operations：活動
interests：利益

under "constant review"：「絶え間ない調査」の対象となる

integrity：完全性

put a stranglehold on ～：～を抑制する
undermine ～：～を損なう

dispenses ～：～を分配する

come to terms with ～：～を理解する
coach：監督
chief lieutenant：首席補佐官
director：代表

# *Exercises*

**Multiple Choice**

次の１～５の英文を完成させるために、a～dの中から最も適切なものを１つ選びなさい。

1. The British government froze Roman Abramovich's assets due to

    **a.** Chelsea's poor performances.

    **b.** Russia's invasion of Ukraine.

    **c.** his dealings on multi-million dollar trading markets.

    **d.** corruption in Russian soccer.

2. The writer states that Chelsea owner Roman Abramovich

    **a.** had been at school with Vladimir Putin.

    **b.** was suspected of close connections with Russia's KGB.

    **c.** was not the only Russian oligarch to be punished.

    **d.** had actively supported the war against Ukraine.

3. Some Chelsea players and coaches were concerned about

    **a.** their unpredictable future.

    **b**. being accused of supporting Putin.

    **c.** Abramovich's declining performance on the field.

    **d.** the influence of Russian television on their club.

4. The British government issued Chelsea a license allowing it to continue

    **a.** spending money as before.

    **b.** competing in the Premier League.

    **c.** playing soccer in empty stadiums.

    **d.** paying staff, but not players.

5. Despite the sanctions, Britain's government considers Chelsea

    **a.** a club dominated by Russians.

    **b.** the best soccer team in Europe.

    **c.** a burden on the economy.

    **d.** of national cultural and economic significance.

本文の内容に合致するものにＴ（True）、合致しないものにＦ（False）をつけなさい。

( ) **1.** Roman Abramovich has had a good friendship with Vladimir Putin.

( ) **2.** Roman Abramovich will sell Chelsea in the near future.

( ) **3.** The British government froze the assets of seven Russian oligarchs.

( ) **4.** Chelsea's players and coaches should still be able to complete their season.

( ) **5.** Only the coach seems to know what the club is allowed to do.

## Vocabulary

次の１～８は、サッカーに関する英文です。下の語群の中から最も適当な語や語句を１つ選び、（　）内に記入しなさい。

1. An attacking player attempts to kick the ball past the (　　　　) team's goalkeeper and between the goalposts to score a goal.

2. A (　　　　) saved a close-range shot from inside the penalty area.

3. A player takes a free kick, while the opposition form a (　　　　) in order to try to deflect the ball.

4. A goalkeeper (　　　　) to stop the ball from (　　　　) his goal.

5. A (　　　　) is when the same player makes three goals in one game.

6. Football is a game played between two teams of (　　　　) players using a round ball.

7. Players are cautioned with a (　　　　) card, and sent off with a (　　　　) card.

8. A player scores a penalty kick given after an offence is committed inside the (　　　　) area.

| dives | eleven | entering | goalkeeper | hat trick |
| opposing | penalty | red | wall | yellow |

- 大谷翔平選手　ア・リーグMVPに誰もが納得
- 大谷翔平選手　「神懸かりな」歴史的夜

大谷翔平選手が米国大リーグ野球のアメリカン・リーグ最優秀選手に満票で選ばれる　The New York Times ／ Redux ／アフロ

## *Before you read*

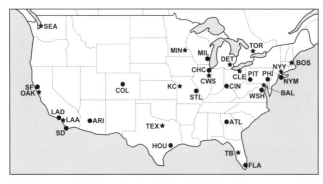

**アメリカンリーグ ★**
**東地区**
Baltimore Orioles（BAL）
Boston Red Sox（BOS）
New York Yankees（NYY）
Tampa Bay Rays（TB）
Toronto Blue Jays（TOR）

**中地区**
Chicago White Sox（CWS）
Cleveland Indians（CLE）
Detroit Tigers（DET）
Kansas City Royals（KC）
Minnesota Twins（MIN）

**西地区**
Los Angeles Angels of Anaheim（LAA）
Oakland Athletics（OAK）
Seattle Mariners（SEA）
Texas Rangers（TEX）

**ナショナルリーグ ●**
**東地区**
Atlanta Braves（ATL）
Florida Marlins（FLA）
New York Mets（NYM）
Philadelphia Phillies（PHI）
Washington Nationals（WSH）

**中地区**
Chicago Cubs（CHC）
Cincinnati Reds（CIN）
Houston Astros（HOU）
Milwaukee Brewers（MIL）
Pittsburgh Pirates（PIT）
St. Louis Cardinals（STL）

**西地区**
Arizona Diamondbacks（ARI）
Colorado Rockies（COL）
Los Angeles Dodgers（LAD）
San Diego Padres（SD）
San Francisco Giants（SF）

次の１〜５の語句の説明として最も近いものをa〜eから１つ選び、（　　）内に記入しなさい。

1. slug （　　）　　　　**a.** position with a good view
2. beat out （　　）　　　　**b.** no longer limited by
3. freed from （　　）　　　　**c.** achieve a victory over
4. perch （　　）　　　　**d.** hit
5. possessed （　　）　　　　**e.** completely and obsessively focused

次の英文は記事の要約です。下の語群から最も適切な語を１つ選び、（　　）内に記入しなさい。

26

Last season Shohei Ohtani was not (　　　　) one of the league's best hitters, but also his team's best pitcher. His Most Valuable Player (　　　　) from the American League (　　　　) his decision to remain a two-way player despite being advised (　　　　) it. And Ohtani has already made up for a (　　　　) start to this season by getting 12 strikeouts against the Astros.

against　　award　　justifies　　only　　slow

　　大谷翔平選手は、1994年７月５日に岩手県奥州市（旧水沢市）生まれの28歳だ。193cmの長身を生かして投手と打者を本格的に行う二刀流選手である。アマチュア時代、日本ハム時代、そしてエンジェルスに入団後も投打に大活躍している。投手としては、右投げで、最速165km/hを記録した。オーバースローから繰り出すストレート、フォークボール、スライダーを投げる。また、野手としても左打ちの外野手で、抜群の長打力はメジャーリーグ開幕後のエンジェルスの３試合連続本塁打を記録した。最長飛距離143mの長打力が称賛された。１塁まで3.8秒台の俊足で、強肩も兼ね備えている。

　　渡米４年目の2021年のアメリカン・リーグ最高殊勲選手MVPに選ばれた。投打の「二刀流」で見せた歴史的な活躍に、投票権を持つ全米野球記者協会の30人の記者全員が１位票を投じる「満票」で選ばれた。渡米１年目には右肘、２年目の左膝の手術を経て、患部の不安が消えた４年目、打者で打率２割５分７厘、46本塁打、100打点、26盗塁、投手で９勝２敗、防御率3.18の成績を残した。さらに、リーグの区別なく活躍した選手を選ぶ「All MLB TEAM」のDH部門でFirst Teamに選ばれた。

　　2022年５月15日のアスレティック戦の５回に指名打者として出場し、大リーグ通算100号本塁打を放った。９月25日現在の打撃通算成績は、打率２割７分、打点92点、本塁打34本。投手としては26試合登板し、14勝、防御率2.47である。

27

# Everyone Agrees: Shohei Ohtani Is the A.L.'s M.V.P.

Shohei Ohtani was extraordinary this season. Ohtani, the Los Angeles Angels' two-way star, smashed 46 home runs, drove in 100 runs and posted a .965 on-base plus slugging percentage, trailing only Toronto's Vladimir Guerrero Jr. in
5 the American League. As if that wasn't impressive enough, Ohtani was also his team's best starting pitcher, amassing a 3.18 earned run average and 156 strikeouts in 130 $^{1}/_{3}$ innings over 23 starts.

28

On Thursday, Ohtani's historic efforts were rewarded with
10 the A.L. Most Valuable Player Award. He joined the former Seattle Mariners star outfielder Ichiro Suzuki, the 2001 A.L. M.V.P., as the only Japanese players in Major League Baseball history to earn the award.

Ohtani received all 30 of the first-place votes for the
15 award, which is presented annually by the Baseball Writers' Association of America. He beat out his fellow finalists, Guerrero, who received 29 second-place votes, and second baseman Marcus Semien, also of the Blue Jays, who received 24 third-place votes.

29

20 Throughout his career, even back in Japan, Ohtani has continually faced skepticism over his ability to remain a two-way player. It is hard enough being an everyday hitter in M.L.B., the top league with the best players in the world, let alone also serving as a starting pitcher.

25 But all along, even after having Tommy John surgery on his throwing elbow, his right, in 2018 and another elbow injury in 2020 forced him to miss nearly two seasons of pitching, he insisted on doing both. In his first season in M.L.B., in 2018 after signing with the Angels, Ohtani won the A.L. Rookie
30 of the Year Award. Freed from the playing-time restrictions

| | |
|---|---|
| A.L. : 米大リーグのアメリカン・リーグ《他にナショナル・リーグがあり、両リーグの優勝チームがワールド・シリーズに出場》 | |
| M.V.P. : 最高殊勲選手賞 | |
| two-way : 投打の二刀流 | |
| 100 runs : 100打点 | |
| on-base plus slugging percentage : 出塁率プラス長打率 | |
| Toronto : トロント・ブルージェイズ | |
| starting pitcher : 先発投手 | |
| amassing 〜 : 〜を記録する | |
| earned run average : 防御率 | |
| strikeouts : (奪)三振 | |
| outfielder : 外野手 | |
| Baseball Writers' Association of America : 全米野球記者協会 | |
| finalists : 決勝戦出場者 | |
| Guerrero : ゲレーロ《48本のホームラン王》 | |
| Marcus Semien : マーカス・セミエン《ホームラン47本》 | |
| skepticism : 懐疑的な見方 | |
| everyday hitter : 常時出場の打者 | |
| let alone 〜 : 〜は勿論のこと | |
| Tommy John surgery : 側副靱帯再建術（肘の腱や靱帯の損傷・断裂に対する手術の様式） | |

imposed by his teams in the past, Ohtani was even better this year.

By James Wagner
*The New York Times, November 21, 2021*

30

## Shohei Ohtani 'was possessed' on historic night

'was possessed'：「神懸かりな」

HOUSTON — Shohei Ohtani was winless with a 5.92 ERA
35 in six starts against the Houston Astros entering Wednesday's start.

HOUSTON：ヒューストン《米国テキサス州最大の都市：NASA（米国航空宇宙局）の施設がある》

Watching the superstar's performance from his perch in the dugout, Los Angeles Angels manager Joe Maddon could feel Ohtani was determined to change his fortunes against the
40 Astros on Wednesday night.

fortunes：運勢

He certainly did that.

The two-way star pitched perfect ball into the sixth inning, tied a career-best with 12 strikeouts and also had two hits and two RBIs to lead the Angels to a 6-0 shutout.

career-best：自己最高

two RBIs：2打点

45 "He was possessed tonight," Maddon said. "That was a virtuoso performance from the beginning. He had a different look about him — and the stuff equaled the look."

virtuoso performance：名人芸

Ohtani's big night gave him his first win of the season after entering the game 0-2 with a 7.56 ERA in his first two starts.
50 He struck out six in a row at one point.

big night：素晴らしい夜

struck out six：6三振を奪った

in a row：連続で

Maddon said it was the best he'd ever seen the 27-year-old pitch.

The reigning AL MVP made history Wednesday before he even took the mound. He batted twice in a six-run first
55 inning as the Angels sent 10 to the plate — that made him the first starting pitcher since at least 1900 to bat twice in the first before throwing a pitch, according to the Elias Sports Bureau.

reigning：現在の、当代の

batted：打席に立った

six-run first inning：初回6得点

plate：ホーム・ベース《つまり打席》

Elias Sports Bureau：エリアス・スポーツ《北米主要リーグの記録を扱うデータ会社》

*The New York Post, April 22, 2022*

# *Exercises*

## Multiple Choice

次の１～５の英文を完成させるために、ａ～ｄの中から最も適切なものを１つ選びなさい。

1. Shohei Ohtani had an amazing season because he

   **a.** received his first career hit in MLB.

   **b.** earned his first win on the mound.

   **c.** was awarded Most Valuable Player.

   **d.** achieved all of the above.

2. Shohei Ohtani is known for

   **a.** being the first major league two-way player since Babe Ruth.

   **b.** his pitches of up to 90 kph.

   **c.** demonstrating wonderful poise.

   **d.** being nervous about pitching.

3. Shohei Ohtani received

   **a.** the N.L. M.V.P. in 2018.

   **b.** the N.L. Rookie of the Year Award in 2019.

   **c.** the A.L. M.V.P. in 2020.

   **d.** the A.L. M.V.P. in 2021.

4. Shohei Ohtani scored twelve strikeouts and two hits and two run batted ins

   **a.** to lose the Astros to 0 score.

   **b.** to lead the Athletics to a shutout.

   **c.** to lose the Athletics to 6 scores.

   **d.** to lead the Angels to 6 scores.

5. The abbreviation ERA stands for

   **a.** equal rights amendment.

   **b.** earned run average.

   **c.** emerging rookie award.

   **d.** excellent record achievement.

本文の内容に合致するものに T （True）、合致しないものに F （False） をつけなさい。

(    ) **1.** Ichiro Suzuki, the former Seattle Mariners infielder, received the 2001 A.L. M.V.P.

(    ) **2.** Ohtani earned six more first-place votes than Marcus Semien.

(    ) **3.** Even in Japan, some people remain skeptical over his talent as a two-way player.

(    ) **4.** Ohtani had Tommy John surgery on his throwing elbow in 2020.

(    ) **5.** Ohtani's game against the Angels made it six stunning performances in a row.

## Vocabulary

次の英文は、The New York Times に掲載された *Japan's Perfect Game Drought Ends With a 19-Strikeout Masterpiece* 『日本の完全試合も 19 奪三振で達成する』 の記事の一部です。下の語群から最も適切なものを 1 つ選び、（   ） 内に記入しなさい。

Roki Sasaki's (     ) game was a long time coming, the first in the Japanese majors since 1994. But the wait turned out to be (     ) it. Sasaki struck out 19 of the 27 men he faced, completing what would have to be described as one of the greatest games ever (     ).

The 6-0 (     ) for the Chiba Lotte Marines over the Orix Buffaloes on Sunday did not only break the Japanese record for (     ) in a perfect game, but it also far (     ) the major league mark of 14 by Matt Cain of the Giants in 2012 and Sandy Koufax for the Dodgers in 1965.

Sasaki, 20, struck out the third batter he faced in the first inning, then struck out the side in the second, third, fourth and fifth innings. The 13 (     ) strikeouts is a Japanese baseball record.

It was the first complete game of Sasaki's young career, and even with the high strikeout total it required only 105 pitches. "The big thing today was getting ahead in counts, being able to throw strikes," Sasaki told Kyodo News. "Now I want to do my (     ) to pitch well next time."

| | | | |
|---|---|---|---|
| best | consecutive | perfect | pitched |
| strikeouts | surpassed | victory | worth |

# ● シンガポール　「不当感」の増大で死刑反対意見強まる

シンガポールの「スピーカーズ・コーナー」で「死刑反対」を訴えるＴシャツ
を着た女性
AFP ／ WAA

## *Before you read*

### Republic of Singapore
### シンガポール共和国
#### 1965年8月9日マレーシアより独立

面積　720km²（東京23区とほぼ同じ）
人口　5,850,000人
民族　中国系　74%／マレー系　14%
　　　インド系　7.9%／その他　1.4%
公用語　国語はマレー語　12.2%
　　　中国語　50%／英語　32.3%
　　　タミル語　3.3%
GDP　3,399億8,100万ドル（世界38位）
　　　1人当たりのGDP　59,795ドル
通貨　シンガポール・ドル
宗教　無宗教信者　17%
　　　仏教　33%／イスラム教　15%
　　　キリスト教　18%／ヒンドゥ教　5％
政体　立憲共和制
識字率　97%

次の1〜5の語句の説明として最も近いものをa〜eから1つ選び、（　）内に記入しなさい。

1. clemency （　　）　　　　　　a. argue against
2. on death row （　　）　　　　b. become friends with
3. fall in with （　　）　　　　　c. waiting to be executed
4. marginalized （　　）　　　　d. outlying and disadvantaged
5. critique （　　）　　　　　　e. mercy

**Summary**

次の英文は記事の要約です。下の語群から最も適切な語を1つ選び、（　）内に記入しなさい。

Singapore continues to (　　　　　) drug-traffickers. The government argues that its (　　　　　) policy keeps people safe. But (　　　　　) about the fairness of the death penalty are growing. On death row for carrying a small quantity of drugs, Nagaenthran Dharmalingam claimed to have been (　　　　　) into crime. His supporters point out that his IQ is very low. But his final appeal was (　　　　　).

| doubts | execute | forced | rejected | severe |

　　シンガポールの領土は、埋立てにより拡大されてきた。事実上1つの都市から構成される都市国家である。教育、娯楽、金融、ヘルスケア、人的資本、イノベーション、物流、製造・技術、観光、貿易・輸送は世界的な中心にある。世界で最も「テクノロジー対応」国家（WEF）、国際会議のトップ都市（UIA）、「投資の可能性が最も高い」都市（BERI）、最も安全な国、最も競争力のある経済などが国際ランキングで上位に格付けされている。さらに、シンガポールは、購買力平価による1人当たり国内総生産（GDP）が世界で2番目に高く、国連人間開発指数で9位である。2020年のシンガポールの一人当たりの実質国民総所得GNIは86,480ドルである。

　　シンガポール島嶼には2世紀に定住が始まり、1400年頃マラッカ王国が建国された。1942年から1945年まで日本軍に占領されたが、1959年にイギリスより自治権を獲得し、自治州になる。1963年にマレーシアが独立し、1965年マレーシアより分離し、シンガポール共和国として独立した。多文化主義及び文化多様性があり、560万人の人口の38%は、永住者及びその他外国籍の人である。シンガポール人は中国系74.1%、マレー系13.4%、インド系9.2%、大部分は2言語使用者であり、第2母語として英語を使用する。

　　シンガポールの法体系はイングランド法を基礎としている。刑事法や取締法規については一般的に厳格であり、身体刑と死刑が実施されている。世界的にも厳しい死刑制度を維持している。薬物に関する犯罪については厳格で、麻薬の密輸で有罪になった時は死刑のみが適用されたため、入国カードにも「麻薬密輸者は死刑」と警告文が書いてある。外国人の麻薬密売業者が死刑になった事例が存在し、死刑廃止国との間で外交問題に発展したことがある。

# *Reading*

33

## Singapore hardens opinion against death penalty as 'sense of injustice' grows

| against 〜：〜反対の |
|---|
| 'sense of injustice'：「不当感」 |

The news was delivered in just a few cold sentences. An appeal for clemency for Nagaenthran Dharmalingam, a man on death row whose case has prompted a global outcry, had failed.

clemency：恩赦
man on death row：死刑囚
outcry：抗議

5　"Please be informed that the position...remains unchanged" wrote Singapore president's principal private secretary, in a letter to Nagaenthran's family: "The sentence of death therefore stands."

sentence of death：死刑判決

stands：有効だ

34

Nagaenthran's relatives and supporters have campaigned
10　tirelessly for his life to be spared. He was arrested in 2009, aged 21, for attempting to smuggle a small amount of heroin — about three tablespoons — into Singapore and has since spent more than a decade on death row. His lawyer has argued that he has an IQ of 69, a level recognised as indicating a
15　learning disability, and should be protected from execution under international law. Nagaenthran has said he was coerced into carrying the drugs.

smuggle 〜 into …：〜を…に密輸する

IQ：知能指数
learning disability：学習障害
execution：死刑執行
coerced into 〜：〜するよう強要される
rights groups：人権団体

Nagaenthran's case has appalled rights groups, and provoked an outcry from voices around the world — from
20　billionaire businessman Richard Branson, a critic of the death penalty, to EU representatives and UN experts. Domestically, it has also prompted some younger Singaporeans to question a system that the government has long claimed makes the city state "one of the safest places in the world".

city state：都市国家《シンガポールのこと》

25　Death penalty cases are rarely reported in any detail in Singapore's tightly controlled media, but Nagaenthran's story has been shared widely online. Isaac Chiew, a 22-year-old university student, said he hadn't thought very much about the death penalty, until he came across Nagaenthran's case on
30　Instagram. "Reading all the details really made me feel this sense of injustice," he says. He began to read about others

Instagram：インスタグラム《写真やビデオを共有するソーシャル・ネットワーキング・サービス》

35

on death row, and was struck by stories of people who were condemned to death simply for falling in with the wrong crowd or making a mistake.

35  Profiles of some death row inmates shared online by campaigners show they are not big time criminals, but rather men from marginalised communities who have faced poverty, or struggled with addiction.

 "Social media has allowed us to centre the voices of death 40 row prisoners and their families," says Jolovan Wham, a human rights activist.

 In a rare protest this month, more than 400 people turned out at Speakers' Corner at Hong Lim park, the only place where demonstrations are permitted in Singapore, to call for 45 executions to be halted.

 Kirsten Han, a journalist and activist who has spent a decade campaigning against the death penalty, believes its likely the highest turn out ever seen at such a demonstration. The message, too, was different.

50  "Previously a lot of other death penalty events might have been focused on - give this person a chance," said Han. But protesters were now critiquing the whole system. They weren't, she added, just expressing pity for any one person; they were calling for abolition of the death penalty. Most of 55 the attendees were young Singaporeans.

 The government argues that capital punishment is the most effective deterrent against crime — an idea debunked by criminological research, she adds.

By Rebecca Ratcliffe
*The Guardian News & Media Ltd, April 13, 2022*

---

condemned to death：死刑宣告される

falling in with ～：～に加わる

inmates：入獄者

big time：一流の、大物の

marginalised：疎外された

addiction：依存症

human rights activist：人権活動家

turned out：集まった

Speakers' Corner：スピーカーズ・コーナー《野外での演説、討論や議論が可能なエリア》

different：今までとは異なる

this：ある特定の、これこれの

They weren't：以前はそうではなかった

abolition：廃止

capital punishment：死刑

deterrent：抑止力

debunked by ～：～によって虚偽だと暴かれる

criminological：犯罪学の

# Exercises

## Multiple Choice

次の、1〜4の英文を完成させ、5の英文の質問に答えるために、a〜dの中から最も適切なものを1つ選びなさい。

1. Capital punishment is _____ in Singapore.

    **a.** no longer used
    **b.** carried out
    **c.** to be reintroduced
    **d.** hardly used

2. Nagaenthran Dharmalingam's case has been globally discussed because of his

    **a.** frequent trafficking in narcotics.
    **b.** long-term addiction to drugs.
    **c.** violent criminal methods.
    **d.** weak mental capacity.

3. Nagaenthran's lawyer claims that _____ violates international law.

    **a.** giving the death penalty to drug-traffickers
    **b.** executing people with learning disabilities
    **c.** keeping prisoners on death row for a decade
    **d.** allowing someone to carry drugs

4. Many death row prisoners come from

    **a.** powerful communities.
    **b.** influential communities.
    **c.** rich communities.
    **d.** powerless communities.

5. Who is described as campaigning against capital punishment for ten years?

    **a.** Richard Branson.
    **b.** Jolovan Wham.
    **c.** Isaac Chiew.
    **d.** Kirsten Han.

本文の内容に合致するものにＴ（True）、合致しないものにＦ（False）をつけなさい。

(   ) **1.** In a letter to Nagaenthran's family, the president's principle private secretary said the death penalty is not in force anymore.

(   ) **2.** Nagaenthran was arrested for taking heroin about three years ago.

(   ) **3.** Nagaenthran's story has spread online in Singapore.

(   ) **4.** Hong Lim Park's Speakers' Corner is one of several places for demonstrations in Singapore.

(   ) **5.** The Singaporean government argues that the death penalty is the most effective measure against crime.

## Vocabulary

次の１～８は、「法律」に関する英文です。日本文に合わせて、適当な語を下の語群から
１つ選び、（　　）内に記入しなさい。

**1.** 彼は、詐欺容疑で逮捕された。
He was (        ) on suspicion of fraud.

**2.** 彼は、有罪と判決が下されたが、すぐに上告した。
He was found (       ) but appealed immediately.

**3.** 彼は、心神喪失の理由で無罪と判決が下された。
He was (       ) by reason of insanity.

**4.** 多くの国は、死刑を廃止した。
Many countries have abolished (      ).

**5.** 地方裁判所は、彼に無期懲役を言い渡した。
The district court sentenced him to (      ).

**6.** 裁判所は、彼に懲役２年、執行猶予３年の判決を下した。
The court gave him two years' imprisonment with a three years'
(      ).

**7.** 死刑が、終身刑に減刑された。
The sentence of death was (      ) into life imprisonment.

**8.** 彼は、刑務所で６年間務めた後で仮釈放された。
He was (       ) after serving 6 years in prison.

| | | | |
|---|---|---|---|
| acquitted | arrested | capital punishment | commuted |
| guilty | life in prison | paroled | stay of execution |

# ●仕事の未来：流行りの職場５選

男性起業家たちが話をしている傍らでパソコンを使い「会社」の仕事をする女性会社員
WESTEND61／アフロ

## *Before you read*

### Questions

**1.** Do you think it is better to work from home or at a workplace?

自宅で仕事をするか、職場で仕事をするか、どちらがいいと思いますか？

**2.** Do you think AI is creating more jobs than it destroys?

AI は壊すよりも多くの雇用を生み出していると思いますか？

次の1～5の語句の説明として最も近いものをa～eから1つ選び、（　　）内に記入しなさい。

1. align with　　　（　　）　　**a.** stability or ability to keep going
2. hot-desking　　（　　）　　**b.** allocating work-stations on a rotating basis
3. resilience　　　（　　）　　**c.** observe or supervise
4. intrusive　　　（　　）　　**d.** conform to
5. oversee　　　　（　　）　　**e.** interfering

次の英文は記事の要約です。下の語群から最も適切な語を1つ選び、（　　）内に記入しなさい。

38

Work (　　　) continue to change. More people will have a choice about where to work, many (　　　) between visiting offices and working remotely. A.I. will become an important tool, while taking (　　　) some jobs entirely. Employers will also have to pay more attention to their workers' physical and (　　　) health. And so employees may find themselves being (　　　) more closely.

alternating　　financial　　monitored　　over　　practices

　　Hybrid working（ハイブリッド・ワーク）とは、リモート勤務とオフィス勤務を柔軟に組み合わせた働き方のことを指す。最近は、オフィスか自宅かだけでなく、シェアオフィスやコーワーキングスペースといった働く場が増えている。ハイブリッド・ワークは新しいワークスタイルとして認知されつつあり、今後主流になると考えられている。このハイブリッド・ワークを進めることにより、良い点、不利な点、さらに今後の課題もあると思われる。
　　まず良い点としては、会社勤務か自宅勤務を自由に選べるため、最適な環境で仕事ができ、生産性の向上が期待できるし、従業員の満足度も上がる。結果的に優秀な人材を確保できる。しかし、不利な点は、家だと会社ほど集中できないし、社内しかできない仕事もある。従来のコミュニケーション方法では意思疎通がしづらくなる。従業員が様々な場所で働いているため、勤怠管理が難しくなり、もともと予定していなかった業務や緊急の会議にも対応しにくくなる。さらに、職場に対しての帰属意識が薄れていく可能性もある。
　　それでは、ハイブリッド・ワークを向上させるために、従来の固定席を廃止して、スペースをもっと自由に使えるようなオフィス環境の整備が必要だ。オフィスのPCをテレワーク用PCから遠隔操作する方式にしたり、オフィスPCを持ち帰る事のできる方式を取り入れたり、また、Web会議システムや勤怠管理システムの導入なども必要だ。さらに、業務を円滑に行うため、ハイブリッド・ワーク導入後もコミュニケーションを意識的に取ることが大切だ。

# Reading

39

## Future Of Work: The 5 Biggest Workplace Trends In 2022

### Hybrid working

When it comes to where we work, there will continue to be three main models — centralized workplaces, decentralized remote organizations, and the hybrid "best of both worlds" approach. What's likely to change in 2022 is that it's more likely that we, as workers, will have the choice rather than being forced to align with whatever model your organization has chosen out of necessity.

Hybrid structures will range from companies maintaining permanent centralized offices with hot-desking to accommodate the fact that staff will more frequently work remotely, to doing away with offices entirely and relying on co-working spaces and serviced meeting rooms to support the needs of a primarily remote workforce.

40

### AI-augmented workforce

The World Economic Forum predicts that AI and automation will lead to the creation of 97 million new jobs by 2025. However, people working in many existing jobs will also find their roles changing, as they are increasingly expected to augment their own abilities with AI technology. Initially, this AI will primarily be used to automate repetitive elements of their day-to-day roles and allow workers to focus on areas that require a more human touch — creativity, imagination, high-level strategy, or emotional intelligence, for example. Some examples include lawyers who will use technology that cuts down the amount of time spent reviewing case histories in order to find precedents, and doctors who will have computer vision capabilities to help them analyze medical records and scans to help them diagnose illness in patients.

41

### Staffing for resilience

Pre-pandemic, the priority was generally to have been

When it comes to ～：～に関しては

decentralized：分散型の

align with ～：～に合わせる

out of necessity：必要に応じて

hot-desking：ホットデスキング《職場で複数の人たちが1つの机やコンピュータなどを共有するシステム》

doing away with ～：～を廃止する

co-working：コワーキング《異なる企業に属する人たちが経費削減のため、1つの事務スペースを共有しながら仕事をすること》

AI-augmented：AI（人工知能）で強化された

World Economic Forum：世界経済フォーラム《ダボスでの賢人会議》

touch：特徴

emotional intelligence：感情的知性《人間関係を上手く維持する能力》

case histories：事例

computer vision：コンピュータ画像

diagnose ～：～を診断する

Staffing：人員配置

resilience：レジリエンス、回復力

generally to have been：一般的には昔からずっとそうだが《挿入と考える》

to hire staff that would create efficient organizations. Mid
35 and post-pandemic, the emphasis has shifted firmly in the
direction of resilience.

This certainly encompasses another sub-trend, which is that
employers are coming to understand the critical importance of
building employee healthcare and wellbeing (including mental
40 health) strategies into their game plan. Many are now trying to
take more responsibility for helping their workforce maintain
physical, mental, and financial wellbeing. A challenge here
that companies will come up against in 2022 is finding ways
to do this that hit objectives without being overly intrusive or
45 invasive of employees' privacy and personal lives.

game plan：作戦、行動計画

challenge：課題

come up against：～に直
面する

42

## Less focus on roles, more focus on skills

Skills are critical because they address core business
challenges, with the competencies needed in a workforce to
50 overcome those challenges. Roles, on the other hand, describe
the way individual members of a workforce relate to an
overall organizational structure or hierarchy. By focussing on
skills, businesses address the fact that solving problems and
answering their core business questions is the key to driving
55 innovation and success within information-age enterprises.

address ～：～に対処する
competencies：能力

hierarchy：階層

driving ～：～を推進する

43

## Employee monitoring and analytics

Controversial though it may be, research shows that
employers are increasingly investing in technology designed
60 to monitor and track the behavior of their employees in order to
drive efficiency. Platforms such as Aware that allow businesses
to monitor behavior across email and tools such as Slack in
order to measure productivity, are being seen as particularly
useful by managers overseeing remote workforces.

By Bernard Marr
*Forbes, November 23, 2021*

monitoring：監視
Controversial though it
may be：物議を醸すかも
知れませんが

Platforms：プラットフォー
ム、（情報配信やビジネス
を行うための）基盤
tools：ツール《プログラム
を作るときなどに使われ
る、小規模なユーティリ
ティ・プログラム》
Slack：《メッセージ・プロ
グラムの一種》
*Forbes*：フォーブス《米国
経済誌》

# *Exercises*

**Multiple Choice**

次の１～５の英文を完成させるために、 a～dの中から最も適切なものを１つ選びなさい。

1. Offices with "hot-desking"

    **a.** have done away with permanent facilities.

    **b.** provide working spaces in remote locations.

    **c.** assume that only some employees come in on some days.

    **d.** guarantee enough desks for all employees.


2. It is predicted that AI will

    **a.** create some new jobs and change some existing jobs.

    **b.** replace doctors and lawyers.

    **c.** mainly perform tasks requiring creativity.

    **d.** only help people doing boring or repetitive work.


3. Post-pandemic, employers will focus on supporting employees'

    **a.** privacy.

    **b.** mental and physical health.

    **c.** personalities.

    **d.** sense of responsibility.


4. Skills are described as more task-oriented, while roles seem to be more

    **a.** happiness-oriented.

    **b.** profit-oriented.

    **c.** organization-oriented.

    **d.** competency-oriented.


5. The increase in remote work means employers are

    **a.** investing in technology to monitor employees.

    **b.** being monitored more by their employees.

    **c.** reluctant to monitor employees out of concern for their privacy.

    **d.** unable to monitor employees outside the office.

本文の内容に合致するものに T （True）、合致しないものに F （False） をつけなさい。

( 　 ) **1.** Tools such as Aware are used by businesses to send emails to employees.

( 　 ) **2.** Employers will focus on roles more than on skills.

( 　 ) **3.** Employers are becoming more interested in employees' healthcare and wellbeing.

( 　 ) **4.** Workers are increasingly expected to enhance their abilities with AI technology.

( 　 ) **5.** The article suggests that work patterns will become less varied.

## Vocabulary

次の１～８は、「働く」に関する英文です。日本文に合わせて、適切な語を下の語群から１つ選び、（　　）内に記入しなさい。

**1.** なりふり構わず働くということは、一生懸命働くことだ。
If you work like a ( 　　 ), you work very hard.

**2.** 骨身を惜しまず働くということは、特に長時間働くということだ。
If you work your ( 　　 ) to the bone, you work extremely hard, especially, for a long time.

**3.** 死ぬまで働くというのはあまり疲れていてもう働くことが出来ないまで働くことだ。
If you work till you ( 　　 ), you work until you are so tired that you cannot work any more.

**4.** あなたは全く仕事中毒人間だ。仕事があなたの全人生だ。
You're a complete ( 　　 ) — your job is your whole life.

**5.** "よく遊び、よく学べ" ということは勉強ばかりしているとつまらない人になるという意味だ。
"All work and no ( 　　 ) makes Jack a dull boy" means that someone who works all of the time will become boring and uninteresting.

**6.** 会社は、我々にテレワークをするように促している。
Our company encourages us to work ( 　　 ).

**7.** 好きなところで働くフリーランスの在宅勤務者だ。
He is a freelance ( 　　 ) who works wherever he wants.

**8.** 学生ローン返済のため20年間働く必要がある。
I need twenty years to work ( 　　 ) my student loans.

| | | | |
|---|---|---|---|
| dog | drop | fingers | off |
| play | remotely | telecommuter | workaholic |

## ●中国　離婚率と結婚率低下

婚姻登録所で結婚証明書を手に、記念写真する若い中国人夫婦　　　　　　AFP／WAA

## *Before you read*

### People's Republic of China
### 中華人民共和国

面積　9,634,057km²（日本の約25倍）（世界4位）
人口　1,433,784,000人（世界1位）
首都　北京／**最大都市**　上海
公用語　中国語
識字率　95.9%
民族　漢族　11億7,000万～12億人（90%～92%）
　　　55の少数民族8%
　　　チワン族（1,600万人）満族（1,000万人）
　　　回族（900万人）ミャオ族（800万人）
　　　ウイグル族・イ族（各700万人）ブイ族（300万人）
宗教　宗教信者　1億人　0.08%／仏教　6.2%
　　　キリスト教　2.3%／道教・無宗教　87.4%
　　　イスラム教　1.7%
GDP　13兆3,680億ドル（世界2位）
　　　1人当たりのGDP　9,580ドル（世界72位）
通貨　元
政体　一党独裁制の社会主義共和国

次の１〜５の語句の説明として最も近いものをａ〜ｅから１つ選び、（　　）内に記入しなさい。

1. undergo　　　　（　　）
2. hail　　　　　　（　　）
3. manageable　　（　　）
4. prerequisite　　（　　）
5. decades-old　　（　　）

a. greet
b. requirement
c. lasting for tens of years
d. be subjected to
e. able to cope with

**Summary**

次の英文は記事の要約です。下の語群から最も適切な語を１つ選び、（　　）内に記入しなさい。

44

（　　　　　　　）Chinese are marrying or having children. Worried about an impending population （　　　　　　　）, the government is emphasizing family values. Couples wanting to divorce must now （　　　　　）for 30 days. This requirement does seem to have （　　　　　）the divorce rate. But the marriage rate is continuing to fall, with many people （　　　　　）pressure from their families to get married.

drop　　fewer　　resisting　　slowed　　wait

中国は、1979年に「一人っ子政策」を導入し、夫婦の子供の数を１人に制限し、２人目から罰金を科したが、2016年に「二人っ子政策」、2021年には「三人っ子政策」を打ち出して、出産奨励に転じた。もし「一人っ子政策」を実施していなかったら、総人口は17億から18億になっていたと言われている。しかし、少子化に歯止めがかからない。国家統計局によると、出生数は、2019年の1465万人、20年1200万人、21年1062万人と毎年減少している。

政府の国家衛生健康委員会は、①20歳から34歳の女性の減少 ②晩婚化が進み、出産意欲も低下 ③出産・子育て・教育コストの高止まりの３点の理由を挙げた。「一人っ子政策」と男子偏重の影響を受け、2021年の20歳から40歳までの結婚適齢期の男女比が108.9対100で明らかに男性の結婚相手が不足している。また意欲的な女性には、仕事と家庭・育児の両立が困難なため、結婚や出産を避ける傾向にある。婚姻件数も2013年には1347万組、以後毎年減少して20年に813万組、21年763万組となり、13年より40％以上も減少している。

中国が「社会主義社会」から「市場経済導入社会」へ変化したため、出産や育児、教育が公的に保障されていたが、現在は個人の負担となった。経済発展の中で競争社会となり、子供の教育、習い事に経済力が問われることとなった。さらに、65歳以上の人口が２億56万人で、総人口14億1260万人の14.2％の割合に拡大し、「高齢化社会」となった。高齢人口の急増は、現役世代や財政の重荷となる。「少子高齢化」は、中国が直面する最大の課題となっている。

## Reading

45

# Divorce Is Down in China, but So Are Marriages

HONG KONG — Faced with a soaring divorce rate, the ruling Communist Party in China introduced a rule last year to keep unhappy marriages together by forcing couples to undergo a 30-day "cooling off" period before finalizing a
5 divorce.

The rule appears to have worked, according to government statistics released this week, which show a steep drop in divorce filings in 2021.

Local officials have hailed the new rule as a success in
10 the country's effort to grow families and curb a demographic crisis threatening China's economy. But the party has a much bigger challenge to reckon with: Fewer and fewer Chinese citizens are getting married in the first place.

46

Along with the decline in the divorce rate, the number of
15 marriage registrations plunged to a 36-year low in 2021. The fall in marriages has contributed to a plummet in birthrates, a worrying sign in China's rapidly graying society and a phenomenon more familiar in countries like Japan and South Korea.

20 Many young Chinese people say they would prefer not to get married, as a job becomes harder to find, competition more fierce and the cost of living less manageable.

47

"I do not want to get married at all," said Yao Xing, a 32-year-old bachelor who lives in the city of Dandong, near
25 China's border with North Korea. His parents are pressuring him to get married and have children, but Mr. Yao said his job buying and selling kitchenware had made it hard to keep a steady income, which he sees as a prerequisite to marriage. Besides, he added, many women don't want to get married
30 anyway.

"I think more and more people around me don't want to get married, and the divorce rate and marriage rate in China

---

Divorce：離婚

So Are 〜：〜もだ《前文（肯定文）の述部を受ける》

soaring：高騰する

introduced 〜：〜を導入した

statistics：統計

divorce filings：離婚届

curb 〜：〜を抑える

demographic crisis：人口動態危機

reckon with 〜：〜を考慮する

in the first place：そもそも

36-year low：36年ぶりの低水準

contributed to 〜：〜の一因となった

graying society：高齢化する社会

prefer not to 〜：〜したくない

bachelor：独身男性

Dandong：丹東

prerequisite to 〜：〜に対する前提条件

have dropped significantly, which I think is an irreversible trend," Mr. Yao said.

35　Rising gender inequality at work and at home has caused many women to think twice about marriage as well. Better educated and more financially independent than their mothers, younger women have watched as their economic position has changed while society's view of them has not.

40　The couples who do get married in China often prefer not to have children, citing worries about the rising cost of education and the burden of taking care of aging parents while also having young children. Some are delaying getting married, choosing instead to live together without the ceremony and,

45　often, without the children.

"The relatively lower marriage rates coupled with rising divorce rates might signal the deinstitutionalization of marriage, which means more people might choose cohabitation over marriage," said Ye Liu, a senior lecturer in the department

50　of international development at King's College London.

Fearful of the day when the population might begin to shrink, the Chinese government has spent years introducing policies to encourage marriage and having children. It has revised strict family planning rules twice in the last decade,

55　first by ending a decades-old "one child" policy in 2015, and later by allowing married couples to have three children.

By Alexandra Stevenson
*The New York Times, March 23, 2022*

irreversible：不可逆的な

think twice：考え直す

watches as 〜：〜するのを見てきた

citing 〜：〜を理由に挙げる

burden：負担

deinstitutionalization：非制度化

choose 〜 over …：…より〜の方を選ぶ

cohabitation：同棲、共同生活

department：学部、学科

King's College London：《ロンドン大学のカレッジの一つ》

shrink：縮小、減少

revised 〜：〜を改訂した

# Exercises

## Multiple Choice

次の１～５の英文を完成させるために、ａ～ｄの中から最も適切なものを１つ選びなさい。

1. The Chinese Communist Party introduced a requirement that couples

   **a.** delay marriage in order to reduce the likelihood of divorce later.

   **b.** refrain from filing for divorce until they have been married for thirty days.

   **c.** experience three weeks of "cooling off" before filing for divorce.

   **d.** wait for thirty days before signing divorce papers.

2. One reason for birthrates plummeting in China is

   **a.** an increase in people delaying their divorce.

   **b.** a decrease in the cost of living.

   **c.** a decrease in marriages.

   **d.** an increase in the age of children.

3. Many Chinese couples do not have children because

   **a.** schooling is getting costly.

   **b.** they may have to care for aging parents.

   **c.** they choose to live together without marrying.

   **d.** of all of the above reasons.

4. Problems that China has include the declining divorce rate and

   **a.** arrival of an aging society.

   **b.** soaring female education.

   **c.** economic growth rate.

   **d.** fierce competition for leadership.

5. The Chinese government's "one-child" policy

   **a.** continues to prevent couples from having children.

   **b.** used to allow couples to have up to three children.

   **c.** was abandoned when population growth slowed.

   **d.** discouraged couples from marrying.

本文の内容に合致するものにＴ（True）、合致しないものにＦ（False）をつけなさい。

(    )   **1.**   The article says that China's population is shrinking.

(    )   **2.**   The decline in marriages has contributed to a rise in birthrates.

(    )   **3.**   Divorce rates have been falling in China for many years.

(    )   **4.**   Falling birthrates used to worry Japan and South Korea more than China.

(    )   **5.**   A falling birthrate will lead to a decline in the number of people of working age.

**Vocabulary**

次の１～６は、結婚や離婚、少子高齢化に関する社会問題を扱った英文です。日本文に合わせて、下の語群から最も適切な語を１つ選び、（   ）内に記入しなさい。

**1.** 結婚したい男性と結婚する気のない女性が、隣同士で座っている。
A man who wants to (      ) and a woman who is not willing to get (      ) sit next to each other.

**2.** 我々夫婦は、協議離婚をすることになった。
My husband and I ended up having a (      ) by (      ).

**3.** 性格の不一致が理由で離婚する夫婦が増えている。
Increasingly more couples are getting (      ) on grounds of (      ).

**4.** 日本社会が抱える問題に少子高齢化がある。
Problems that Japan has include the (      ) birthrate and (      ) society.

**5.** 社会保障制度を充実させる必要がある。
The social (      ) system should be enhanced.

**6.** 国籍や性別、職業などで人を差別してはいけない。
Do not (      ) against people based on nationality, gender or occupation.

| | | | | |
|---|---|---|---|---|
| aging | consent | declining | discriminate | divorce |
| divorced | incompatibility | married | marry | security |

## ●スリランカ　有機農法を始めて大惨事に

経済危機に陥ったスリランカのコロンボで野菜を買い求める人々　　　AFP／WAA

## *Before you read*

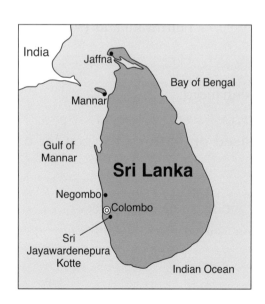

Democratic Socialist Republic of Sri Lanka
### スリランカ民主社会主義共和国

面積　65,610km²（北海道の約0.8倍）
首都　スリ・ジャヤワルダナプラ・コッテ
公用語　シンハラ語・タミル語
人口　21,920,000人
民族　シンハラ人　74.9%／タミル人　15.3%
　　　スリランカ・ムーア人　9.3%
宗教　仏教　70.1%／ヒンドゥ教　12.6%
　　　イスラム教　9.7%／キリスト教　7.6%
識字率　92.5%
GDP　807億米ドル
　　　1人当たりGDP　3,682米ドル
通貨　ルピー
政体　共和制

次の１～５の語の説明として最も近いものをa～eから１つ選び、（　）内に記入しなさい。

**1.** pesticide　　（　　）　　**a.** harvest or gather

**2.** reap　　　　（　　）　　**b.** soar

**3.** spiral　　　（　　）　　**c.** chemical used to destroy bugs

**4.** reversal　　（　　）　　**d.** unblock

**5.** unsnarl　　（　　）　　**e.** adoption of an earlier policy

## Summary

次の英文は記事の要約です。下の語群から最も適切な語を１つ選び、（　）内に記入しなさい。

50

Sri Lanka's government said it stopped importing chemical fertilizers to make food (　　　). Some people, however, think the main (　　　) was to save money. Lockdowns and the (　　　) of tourism hit the local economy badly and limited funds for imports. Unfortunately, organic farming seems to have reduced agricultural (　　　). Food prices have (　　　), and the government has had to reverse its decision.

safer　　soared　　reason　　suspension　　yields

スリランカ共和国は、インド洋の真珠とも言われる緑豊かな熱帯の島で、面積は北海道の約８割。紅茶の生産が盛んで、主要産業は農業と繊維業。人口は約2,167万人、最大都市はコロンボ、首都はスリ・ジャヤワルダナプラ・コッテである。1948年にイギリスから自治領セイロンとして独立。1972年にはスリランカ共和国に改称し、英連邦内の共和国となった。公用語はシンハラ語とタミル語で、国民の¾がシンハラ人で構成され、国民の７割が仏教徒（上座部仏教）である。

スリランカは経常赤字の拡大と輸入インフレの加速が進み、深刻な経済危機に直面している。外貨不足により資源や食糧などの輸入が困難になったことが背景にある。以前から多額の債務を抱えている点で経済構造が脆弱であり、いつ危機に直面してもおかしくないと指摘されてきた。スリランカは2000年代以降、自国での資金調達が難しいことから対外借入を拡大することでインフラ投資を実施し、高成長を目指した。しかし、2017年には融資の返済に行き詰まったことから、中国企業にハンバントタ港の運営権を99年間、引き渡さざるを得なくなるなど、いわゆる「債務のわな」に陥った。さらに、新型コロナ感染拡大によって観光業が低迷し、外貨の獲得が困難となった。ウクライナ問題に端を発する輸入価格上昇が加わり、化学肥料輸入禁止し、有機農業を推進したが、経済危機を免れることができない。2022年７月14日大統領はシンガポールへ逃亡し、辞表を出した。

# Reading

51

## Sri Lanka's Plunge Into Organic Farming Brings Disaster

RATNAPURA, Sri Lanka — This year's crop worries M.D. Somadasa. For four decades, he has sold carrots, beans and tomatoes grown by local farmers using foreign-made chemical fertilizers and pesticides, which helped them reap
5 bigger and richer crops from the verdant hills that ring his hometown.

Then came Sri Lanka's sudden, and disastrous, turn toward organic farming. The government campaign, ostensibly driven by health concerns, lasted only seven months. But
10 farmers and agriculture experts blame the policy for a sharp drop in crop yields and spiraling prices that are worsening the country's growing economic woes and leading to fears of food shortages.

Prices for some foodstuffs, like rice, have risen by nearly
15 one-third compared with a year ago, according to Sri Lanka's central bank. The prices of vegetables like tomatoes and carrots have risen to five times their year-ago levels.

Late last month, Sri Lanka's plantation minister, Ramesh Pathirana, confirmed a partial reversal of the policy, telling the
20 country's Parliament that the government would be importing fertilizer necessary for tea, rubber and coconut, which make up the nation's major agricultural exports.

"We will be importing fertilizers depending on the requirement in the country," Mr. Pathirana told The New York
25 Times. "So far, we don't have enough chemical fertilizers in the country because we didn't import them."

Food costs are rising around the world as pandemic-related supply chain knots are slowly unsnarled and as prices rise for feedstocks like natural gas that are used to make fertilizer and
30 other supplies. Sri Lanka added to those pressures with its own missteps.

| | |
|---|---|
| Sri Lanka：スリランカ《インド南のインド洋にあるセイロン島の国》 | |
| Plunge Into ～：急に～し始めること | |
| Organic Farming：有機農法 | |
| Disaster：大惨事 | |
| crop：収穫高 | |
| fertilizers：肥料 | |
| pesticides：殺虫剤 | |
| prices：物価 | |
| leading to ～：～を引き起こす | |
| by：《程度を表す》 | |
| reversal：失敗、撤回 | |
| make up ～：～を構成する | |
| requirement：要求 | |
| Food costs：食品価格 | |
| feedstocks：原材料 | |
| supplies：生活必需品 | |
| added to ～ with …：…で～を増大させた | |

52

53

Chemical fertilizers are essential tools for modern agriculture. Still, governments and environmental groups have grown increasingly concerned about their overuse. They
35 have been blamed for growing water pollution problems, while scientists have found increased risks of colon, kidney and stomach cancer from excessive nitrate exposure.

President Gotabaya Rajapaksa cited health concerns when his government banned the importation of chemical fertilizers
40 in April, a pledge he had initially made during his 2019 election campaign.

"Sustainable food systems are part of Sri Lanka's rich sociocultural and economic heritage," he told a United Nations summit in September.
45 Mr. Rajapaksa's critics pointed to another reason: Sri Lanka's dwindling reserves of money.

Covid-19 lockdowns devastated Sri Lanka's tourist industry, which generates one-tenth of the country's economic output and provides a major source of foreign currency. The
50 domestic currency, the rupee, has lost about one-fifth of its value, limiting Sri Lanka's ability to purchase food and supplies abroad just as prices were rising. That added to lingering problems like its huge debt load, including on high-interest loans from Chinese state banks that required it to take
55 out still more loans.

"Our annual earnings from tourism amounting to almost $5 billion did not materialize during the last two years," Basil Rajapaksa, the finance minister and the president's brother, told Parliament last month. "As a government, we
60 acknowledge that our foreign reserves are being challenged."

As Sri Lanka's economy struggled and global prices rose, its foreign exchange reserves shrank by about 70 percent. Shaving foreign-made fertilizer from the country's shopping list would help stem the slide.

By Aanya Wipulasena and Mujib Mashal
*The New York Times, December 7, 2021*

water pollution：水質汚染

nitrate exposure：硝酸塩露出

reserves of money：準備金

Covid-19：新型コロナウイルス感染症による

economic output：経済産出量

debt load：借金

including on 〜：〜に書き入れる

take out loans：融資を受ける

materialize：具現化する、実現する

foreign reserves：外貨準備高

challenged：欠けている、足りない

foreign exchange reserves：外貨準備高、外国為替予備金

stem the slide：滑落を食い止める

# Exercises

## Multiple Choice

次の１〜５の英文を完成させるために、a〜dの中から最も適切なものを１つ選びなさい。

1. In April 2019, Sri Lanka banned the import of chemical fertilizers
    a. to raise crop yields.
    b. because pesticides destroy bugs.
    c. to make food safer.
    d. because of soaring food prices.

2. Since the move to organic farming, carrots
    a. have become five times costlier.
    b. are up to one-third pricier.
    c. are even more expensive than tomatoes.
    d. can no longer be imported.

3. _____ hit Sri Lankan tourism badly.
    a. Drops in crop yields
    b. Soaring prices
    c. The falling rupee
    d. Covid lockdowns

4. Some critics say the government was more interested in _____ than promoting healthy farming.
    a. saving money
    b. promoting tourism
    c. raising crop yields
    d. borrowing money from China

5. The Sri Lankan currency, the rupee,
    a. has fallen by around 50%.
    b. has lost nearly one-fourth of its value.
    c. has gone down by about 20%.
    d. has weakened five times.

本文の内容に合致するものにT（True）、合致しないものにF（False）をつけなさい。

( ) **1.** The Sri Lankan government suddenly stopped exporting chemical fertilizers to save money.

( ) **2.** President Gotabaya Rajapaksa discussed health issues during his election campaign.

( ) **3.** There is no risk of colon cancer from chemical fertilizers.

( ) **4.** The economic crisis made the government completely reverse its policy on fertilizers.

( ) **5.** The government has been heavily in debt recently.

**Vocabulary**

次の1～8は「農業」に関する語句です。該当する英語説明文を下のa～hの中から1つ選び、（　）に入れなさい。

1. agriculture ( )
2. chemical fertilizer ( )
3. crop-dusting ( )
4. dairy farming ( )
5. horticulture ( )
6. nursery ( )
7. organic farming ( )
8. pesticide ( )

**a.** a chemical substance added to soil to make it more fertile
**b.** a chemical substance used to kill small animals or insects harming food supplies
**c.** sprinkling insecticide on crops from the air
**d.** growing crops or raising animals for food
**e.** the practice or science of growing fruit, flowers and vegetables
**f.** a method of farming in which food is grown without the help of artificial substances
**g.** the business of producing, storing and distributing milk and its products
**h.** a place where plants and trees are reared for sale or transplantation

# Unit 10

## ●ベンガル湾で大洪水　住民はマングローブの森に避難

インド、増水被害軽減に向け、マングローブの
植林に従事する女性たち
The New York Times／Redux／アフロ

## *Before you read*

### Republic of India　インド共和国

面積　3,287,590km²（日本の8.7倍）（世界７位）
人口　1,310,000,000人（世界２位）
首都　ニューデリー／デリー連邦直轄地
最大都市　ムンバイ
公用語　英語、ヒンドゥ語／識字率　75.6%
民族　インド・アーリア族　72%
　　　ドラヴィダ族　25%／モンゴロイド族　３%
宗教　ヒンドゥ教　79.8%／イスラム教　14.2%
　　　キリスト教　2.3%／シーク教　1.7%
　　　仏教　0.7%／ジャイナ教　0.4%
GDP　２兆7,187億米ドル（世界７位）
　　　１人当たりGDP　2,038米ドル（世界144位）
通貨　インド・ルピー
政体　共和制

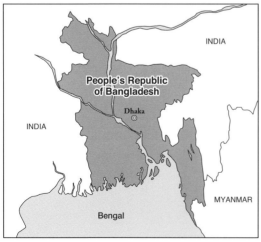

### People's Republic of Bangladesh
### バングラディシュ人民共和国

面積　215,000km²（日本の約40%）
人口　164,680,000人
公用語　ベンガル語／識字率　72.9%
首都　ダッカ
民族　ベンガル人が大部分
宗教　イスラム教　90.4%
　　　ヒンドゥ教・仏教・キリスト教　9.6%
GDP　2,149億米ドル
　　　１人当たりGDP　1,968米ドル
通貨　タカ
政体　共和制

次の1〜5の語句の説明として最も近いものをa〜eから1つ選び、（　）内に記入しなさい。

1. straddle （　　）     **a.** spread across two sides/countries
2. bolster （　　）     **b.** in imminent danger of
3. salinity （　　）     **c.** reinforce
4. nurture （　　）     **d.** help something small grow bigger
5. on the edge of （　　）     **e.** saltiness

**Summary**

次の英文は記事の要約です。下の語群から最も適切な語を1つ選び、（　）内に記入しなさい。

56

    In tropical coastal areas, mangrove forests lower the (　　　　) of flooding by weakening waves. They also (　　　　) greenhouse gases. So, after a powerful cyclone hit the Sundarbans, local inhabitants (　　　　) the advice of conservationists and started planting mangrove (　　　　). Most of the activists are women, and as well as (　　　　) their villages they have found ways to increase their incomes.

followed     protecting     reduce     risk     saplings

    スンダルバンス国立公園（Sundarbans National Park）は、インド共和国・西ベンガル州に所在する国立公園。世界最大規模を有するデルタ地帯の一画を占め、数多くの希少種や絶滅危惧種が生息している。この国立公園は、バングラデシュとの国境に近いインド東部の西ベンガル州南端に所在し、ベンガル湾の奥にひろがる東西およそ250km、南北40〜80kmにおよぶ、世界最大のデルタ（三角州）地帯のなかに立地する。ヒマラヤ山脈より流下するガンジス川とブラマプトラ川は、数百万年前から山地より大量の土砂を運んで下流に巨大な堆積平野を形成してきた。デルタ地帯は表面積80,000km²に及び、川は天然の水路となって網目状に入り組んでいる。

    デルタを形成する水路の沿岸には世界最大規模のマングローブの密林が広がっており、これは当地方に多数発生する暴風雨に対する自然の防波堤の役目を担っている。また、干潮の際にすがたを見せるマングローブの強力な気根は、水中の土砂の流出を食い止めて陸地を形成するのに大きく作用してきた。大河によって運ばれてきた泥はマングローブの根のあいだに厚く堆積してきたのである。なお、スンダルバンス国立公園に近接するバングラデシュ側のシュンドルボンも1997年、世界遺産に登録された。マングローブの密生する湿地帯には300種を超える植物が生育し、数多くの水生・陸生動物のすみかとなっている。また、干潟は上流より運ばれてきた養分豊かな土壌となっているため、数多くの海洋動物はここで孵化期を過ごしている。

## Reading

# Facing Disastrous Floods, They Turned to Mangrove Trees for Protection

     LAKSHMIPUR, India — As sea levels rise, eroding embankments and pushing water closer to their doorsteps, the residents of the hundreds of villages in the Sundarbans — an immense network of rivers, tidal flats, small islands and vast
5 mangrove forests straddling India and Bangladesh — have found their lives and livelihoods at risk.

     In the absence of much government support, women like Aparna Dhara, with help from a nonprofit environmental conservation organization, have devised their own solution:
10 planting hundreds of thousands of additional mangrove trees to bolster their role as protective barriers.

58

     After Cyclone Aila slammed into the region in 2009, causing floods and mudslides, nearly 200 people lost their lives.

15      Amid the rising waters, crocodiles have begun entering villages. And higher salinity in the water has killed off fish "as if the entire area had been crushed under the thumb," said Ajanta Dey, a Kolkata-based conservationist.

     A few years ago, as Ms. Dey went around documenting the
20 post-cyclone wreckage, women like Ms. Dhara approached her and pointed to areas where their homes had once stood. Ms. Dey suggested planting more mangroves between existing embankments and open water. By 2015, over 15,000 women had signed up to for the mission, according to Ms.
25 Dey, program director at Nature Environment and Wildlife Society.

     While all are welcome to participate, many men from the Sundarbans migrate to cities for work, meaning it's the villages' women who are often leading the climate change
30 fight.

     The women, drawing on their deep knowledge of

---

LAKSHMIPUR：《インドのオリッサ州コラブット地方にある都市》

eroding 〜：〜を侵食する

embankments：堤防

tidal flat：干潟

straddling 〜 and …：〜と…とに跨る

at risk：危険に曝されている

nonprofit environmental conservation organization：非営利の環境保護団体

solution：解決方法

mudslides：土砂崩れ

salinity：塩分濃度

documenting 〜：〜を記録する

wreckage：残骸

open water：開放水域

signed up to for 〜：〜に登録した

Nature Environment and Wildlife Society：自然環境及び野生生物協会

it's 〜 that：《強調構文》

drawing on 〜：〜を利用する

the Sundarbans, make hand-drawn maps of areas where mangroves can be planted. They nurture seeds into saplings and then, in baskets or on boats, transport the young trees
35 and dig in the mud flats to plant them. Later, they track their growth on a mobile app.

60

In Ms. Dhara's village, Lakshmipur, the number of acres covered with mangroves has grown to 2,224 from 343 in the last decade. In areas that had been barren-looking mud flats
40 just a few years ago, cranes, gulls and herons abound in the flat rounded leaves of the mangrove trees.

Mangroves, found only in tropical and subtropical climates, are distinctive for their ability to survive in brackish water. Research has shown mangrove forests to be an excellent
45 way to mitigate the effects of climate change, especially the storm surge accompanying cyclones, by reducing the height and speed of waves. Mangroves also help reduce greenhouse gases, as they have high rates of carbon capture.

61

While many in the village share her sense of living on
50 the edge of a climate disaster, Ms. Dhara said it nonetheless seemed impossible at first to persuade her family to let her join the group of women planting mangroves back in 2013.

But Ms. Dhara persisted, and was able to convince her family that the trees would not only help keep the village safe
55 from floods, but were also a chance to earn extra income. Ms. Dey's organization pays the women for growing and planting mangrove saplings, and also helps them sell fish, vegetables, honey, eggs and other local goods.

By Suhasini Raj

*The New York Times, April 10, 2022*

| | |
|---|---|
| nurture 〜 into … : 〜を育てて…にする | |
| saplings : 苗木、若木 | |
| acres : エーカー《面積単位で約4,000㎡》 | |
| abound in 〜 : 〜に沢山いる | |
| distinctive for 〜 : 〜が特徴だ | |
| brackish water : 汽水 | |
| mitigate 〜 : 〜を緩和させる | |
| storm surge : 高潮 | |
| accompanying 〜 : 〜に伴う | |
| rates of carbon capture : 炭素吸収率 | |
| on the edge of 〜 : 〜の危機に瀕して | |
| persuade 〜 to … : …するように〜を説得する | |
| persisted : 何度も粘って主張した | |
| convince 〜 that … : …だと〜を納得させる | |
| extra income : 副収入 | |

# Exercises

次の1〜5の英文を完成させるために、a〜dの中から最も適切なものを1つ選びなさい。

1. The village women decided to

    a. plant mangrove trees to attract tourism.
    b. plant mangrove trees to protect themselves from floods.
    c. dig embankments to deter crocodiles.
    d. dig embankments to provide extra income.

2. In 2009, Cyclone Aila caused floods, and _____ began entering villages.

    a. crocodiles
    b. dead fish
    c. gulls
    d. cranes

3. The women in the Sundarbans _____ mangrove seeds into saplings and then carry the young trees and _____ them into the mud flats.

    a. educate ～ plant
    b. train ～ plant
    c. nurture ～ dig
    d. plant ～ nurture

4. The article states that mangroves are found in tropical and subtropical climates in

    a. sweet water.
    b. clear water.
    c. salty water.
    d. running water.

5. Mangrove forests can _____ and reduce greenhouse gases.

    a. increase the effects of floods
    b. decrease the supply of fish
    c. raise threats from wildlife
    d. lessen harm from climate warming

本文の内容に合致するものに T （True）、合致しないものに F （False）をつけなさい。

(    ) **1.** Ms. Dhara planted mangrove trees because they would not only protect the village from floods but also bring extra income for women.

(    ) **2.** The Sundarbans women planted pine trees for protection against floods and erosion.

(    ) **3.** Mangroves now cover 2,224 more acres in Lakshmipur than before.

(    ) **4.** The women used their local knowledge to produce maps of where mangroves could be planted.

(    ) **5.** The replanting project emerged from meetings between village women and Ms. Dey.

## Vocabulary

　次の 1 〜 7 は、日本語の「植え付ける」を使った語句です。日本文に合わせて、下の語群から最も適切なものを 1 つ選び、（　　）内に記入しなさい。

1. 子供たちに責任感を植え付ける
   （　　　　　　　） children a sense of responsibility

2. 子供たちの心に彼の名前を植え付ける
   （　　　　　　　） his name in the heart of children

3. 子供たちに相互尊重の念を植え付ける
   （　　　　　　　） mutual respect among children

4. 子供たちに一体感を植え付ける
   （　　　　　　　） a feeling of unity in children

5. 子供たちに地球温暖化の恐ろしさを植え付ける
   （　　　　　　　） fear of global warming in children

6. ウイルスを彼のコンピュータに植え付ける
   （　　　　　　　） a virus on his computer

7. 彼の心に疑いの種を植え付ける
   （　　　　　　　） a seed of doubt in his mind

| build | carve | give | instill |
|-------|-------|------|---------|
| plant | put | sow | |

# ● トルコで超インフレとの戦い

物価高の中でトルコ中央銀行が利下げを実施し、インフレがさらに進み、パンも値上がりで庶民は大打撃
AP／アフロ

## *Before you read*

### Republic of Turkey
### トルコ共和国
#### 1923年10月29日共和制宣言

面積　780,576km²（日本の約２倍）
人口　83,614,362人
首都　アンカラ
最大都市　イスタンブール
公用語　トルコ語
識字率　95.6%
民族　トルコ人、アルメニア人、
　　　ユダヤ人、クルド人
宗教　イスラム教・スンニ派　99%
GDP　7,170億米ドル
　　　１人当たり GDP　8,599米ドル
通貨　トルコ・リラ
政体　共和制

次の１〜５の語句の説明として最も近いものをa〜eから１つ選び、（　）内に記入しなさい。

1. wrench out　　（　　）　　a. laugh
2. chuckle　　　（　　）　　b. make even worse
3. crush　　　　（　　）　　c. cause to collapse
4. expansionary　（　　）　　d. pull away by force
5. compound　　（　　）　　e. ambitious and aimed at growth

**Summary**

次の英文は記事の要約です。下の語群から最も適切な語を１つ選び、（　）内に記入しなさい。

62

Turkey's (　　　) has halved in value. And now its people are (　　　) the highest inflation in twenty years. One baker says his customers are (　　　) about his prices. But he himself has to pay (　　　) as much for flour. While Turkey is not the only country with inflation, government economic policies seem to have made it worse than (　　　).

complaining　　currency　　elsewhere　　facing　　twice

　　トルコ共和国は、西アジアに位置するアナトリア半島（小アジア）と東ヨーロッパに位置するバルカン半島東南端の東トラキア地方を領有する共和制国家。首都はアナトリア中央部のアンカラ。アジアとヨーロッパの２つの大陸にまたがる。11世紀にトルコ系のイスラム王朝の支配の下、イスラム教徒のトルコ人が流入するようになり、土着の諸民族と対立・混交しつつ次第に定着していった。オスマン朝は、15世紀にビザンツ帝国を滅ぼしてイスタンブールを都とし、東はアゼルバイジャンから西はモロッコまで、北はウクライナから南はイエメンまで支配する大帝国を打ち立てる。帝国は、第一次世界大戦で敗北し、英仏伊、ギリシャなどの占領下に置かれ、完全に解体された。1924年に西洋化による近代化を目指すイスラム世界初の世俗主義国家トルコ共和国を建国した。第二次世界大戦後は、ソ連の南部に接するため、反共の防波堤として西側世界に迎えられ、1952年にはNATOに、また1961年にはOECDに加盟した。
　　イスラムの復活を望む人々の国内の反体制的な勢力を政治から排除しつつ、西洋化に邁進してきたが、EUへの加盟にはクルド問題やキプロス問題、ヨーロッパ諸国の反トルコ・イスラム感情などが障害となっている。2018年のGDPは約7,700億ドルで、世界第19位、１人あたりのGDPは9,405ドルである。2022年２月のロシアのウクライナ侵攻に伴うエネルギーや食糧品価格高騰が直撃し、コロナ禍からの景気回復に水を差している。トルコの３月の消費者物価上昇率は、前年の３月比で61.14%だった。しかし、低金利で生産を増やし、経済が成長すれば、物価も安定すると考え、金融緩和を続けて来ているが、インフレは止まらない。

63

# Turkey's war with inflation:
## 'Prices change daily and everyone is scared'

scared：怯えている

From behind the counter in a bakery in Kasımpaşa, a working-class Istanbul neighbourhood, Mustafa Kafadar can see the orange, white and blue banners of Recep Tayyip Erdoğan's Justice and Development party (AKP) as they blow
5　in the spring breeze.

Kafadar has been wrenched out of retirement by Turkey's economic crisis — his pension is no longer enough to cover his basic expenses. Now he works shifts in the bakery, where he describes living from payday to payday while he sweeps
10　crumbs off a tray.

64

"Everything's very expensive. After I buy my essentials and pay my bills, there's nothing left," he says.

Asked who is responsible, he chuckles darkly. "You know who makes inflation high," he says cryptically, reluctant to
15　voice his opinion of Erdoğan's economic policies directly.

Turkey is weathering an unprecedented financial crisis. After the lira lost half its value last year alone, the country is now struggling with rocketing inflation, officially 61.14%.

Kafadar arranges rows of delicate breakfast pastries —
20　fluffy round *açma* filled with olives or chocolate, *börek* and glossy *poğaça* buns — as customers arrive. He tells me they sometimes fly into a rage with him about prices. Jars of pink and white sugared almonds and an entire counter of elegant layer cakes, decorated with fruit and chocolate, sit untouched,
25　now a little too pricey for most.

65

"Sugar and wheat prices have gone up. A kilogram bag of flour was 110 lira [£6.15] back in January; now it's 220 lira," he says. Pointing at some of the cheapest buns, he adds: "We couldn't make the prices of the *poğaças* any higher, as people
30　can't afford it."

When Turkey's official inflation rate broke 50% in

Istanbul：イスタンブールにある《トルコ最大の都市：首都はアンカラ》

neighbourhood：地域、区域《working-class が修飾》

Justice and Development party：公正発展党

wrenched out of retirement：引退から身をもぎ取られた→引退できず働かざるを得ない

pension：年金

expenses：支出

works shifts：シフト勤務で働く

living from payday to payday：給料ギリギリの暮らし

bills：請求書

cryptically：謎めかして

reluctant to ～：～するのを躊躇して

weathering ～：～を切り抜けようとしている

lira：トルコ・リラ《トルコの貨幣通貨》

delicate：おいしい

pastries：ペストリー《パイやタルトなど》

fly into a rage：烈火のごとく怒りだす

layer cakes：レイヤー・ケーキ《幾つかの層を重ねて作ったケーキ》

broke ～：～を突破した

February, it represented both a two-decade high and a huge political problem for the government. The finance minister, Nureddin Nebati, insisted earlier this month that the surge
35 was "temporary", while Erdoğan recently vowed to protect Turks against inflation.

"As the Turkish economy is getting ready to become one of the world's top 10 economies, we have said that we will not waste this opportunity with careless and thoughtless steps,"
40 he said. "We will get out of this situation in a way that will not crush our citizens with inflation."

Spiralling inflation is tied to the government's efforts to radically overhaul the Turkish economy, keeping interest rates low in the belief that this will stimulate it and increase
45 production — against the advice of most experts.

"Yes, everyone is experiencing inflation worldwide, but Turkey is experiencing it at almost four or five times the rate of others," says Alp Erinç Yeldan, an economist at Istanbul's Kadir Has University.

50 "This is after a series of policy mistakes and ambitious expansionary projects, including following an economic policy that evades the rules of gravity."

The independent economic research group Enag, which monitors Turkey's inflation rate using the same metrics as the
55 government, calculates real inflation was 142.63% in March.

Turkey's financial crisis has been further compounded by Russia's invasion of Ukraine, which has driven up global food prices, particularly for wheat.

By Ruth Mitchelson and Deniz Barış Narh
*The Guardian News & Media Ltd, April 16, 2022*

"temporary"：「一時的」

ready to ～：今にも～しそうだ

steps：道のり

overhaul ～：～を見直す
interest rates：金利、利率

after ～：～の結果だ

expansionary：拡大経済の、インフレの

evades ～：～から逃れる
gravity：重力
independent：（国や特定組織から）独立した
Enag：エナグ《インフレ研究グループ》
metrics：指標
compounded：悪化させられた
driven up ～：～を押し上げた

# Exercises

**Multiple Choice**

次の1～5の英文を完成させるために、a～dの中から最も適切なものを1つ選びなさい。

1. Kafadar's pension

    **a.** allows him to enjoy retirement.

    **b.** is too small for him to live without working.

    **c.** just covers his basic expenses.

    **d.** enabled him to buy a bakery.

2. In 2021, the Turkish lira

    **a.** recovered one third of its value.

    **b.** lost half its value.

    **c.** recovered half its value.

    **d.** lost a quarter of its value.

3. Turkey's finance minister emphasized that

    **a.** inflation was rocketing.

    **b.** economic problems would continue into next year.

    **c.** deflation was a bigger problem than inflation.

    **d.** the economic crisis was temporary.

4. The Turkish government believed that _____ would augment production and help the economy _____.

    **a.** high interest rates ～ grow

    **b.** high interest rates ～ advance

    **c.** low interest rates ～ go backward

    **d.** low interest rates ～ expand

5. Turkey's financial problems have been worsened by

    **a.** Covid-19.

    **b.** Russia's invasion of Ukraine.

    **c.** global inflation.

    **d.** the fall of Erdoğan's government.

本文の内容に合致するものにＴ（True）、合致しないものにＦ（False）をつけなさい。

(    ) **1.** War overseas has helped drive up the price of goods that bakeries buy.

(    ) **2.** Turkey's government is in no way the cause of inflation there.

(    ) **3.** Kafadar openly criticized the Turkish president's economic policies.

(    ) **4.** Few customers at Kafadar's store buy jars of sugared almonds because of the price.

(    ) **5.** The Kadir Has economist explained how inflation in other countries is just as bad as in Turkey.

## Vocabulary

次の１～８の語句は、経済に関する反意語です。(   ) 内に最も適切な下のａ～ｈの語群、また ［   ］ 内に下のＡ～Ｈの日本語句の説明に入れなさい。

1. devaluation ［    ］    ↔    (    )［平価切上げ］
2. (    ) market［強気市場］    ↔    bear market ［    ］
3. inflationary spiral ［    ］    ↔    (    ) spiral［デフレスパイラル］
4. yen's (    )［円安］    ↔    yen's appreciation ［    ］
5. credit (    )［金融引き締め］    ↔    credit relaxation ［    ］
6. trade deficit ［    ］    ↔    trade (    )［貿易収支黒字］
7. economic (    )［不景気］    ↔    economic booming ［    ］
8. creditor country ［    ］    ↔    (    ) country［債務国］

| | | |
|---|---|---|
| **a.** bull | **A.** インフレスパイラル | |
| **b.** depreciation | **B.** 円高 | |
| **c.** debtor | **C.** 金融緩和 | |
| **d.** deflationary | **D.** 好景気 | |
| **e.** revaluation | **E.** 債権国 | |
| **f.** slumping | **F.** 平価切下げ | |
| **g.** squeeze | **G.** 貿易収支赤字 | |
| **h.** surplus | **H.** 弱気市場 | |

# Unit 12

## ●韓国での「多文化主義」とは

韓国・大邱でイスラム教モスク建設を巡り建築主と地元住民が対立。
「多文化主義」とは？　　　　　　　　The New York Times ／ Redux ／アフロ

## *Before you read*

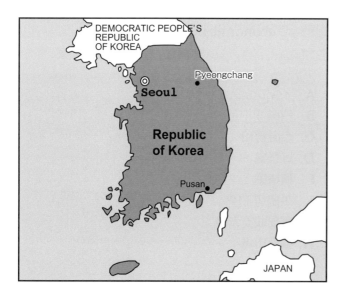

### Republic of Korea （South Korea）
### 大韓民国

38度線を挟み朝鮮民主主義人民共和国の統治区域
と対峙する分断国家である

面積　100,210km²（日本の約４分の１）（世界107位）
人口　51,830,000人（世界28位）
民族　大半が朝鮮民族
首都　ソウル
公用語　朝鮮語
宗教　キリスト教・カトリック　20.6%
　　　キリスト教・プロテスタント　34.5%
　　　仏教　42.9%
GDP　１兆6,308億米ドル（世界10位）
　　　１人当たりの GDP　33,320米ドル（世界28位）
通貨　ウォン
政体　民主共和制
識字率　99%

## Words and Phrases

次の１～５の語句の説明として最も近いものをa～eから１つ選び、（　）内に記入しなさい。

| | | | |
|---|---|---|---|
| **1.** a den of | （　） | **a.** | the worst or heaviest burden |
| **2.** expose | （　） | **b.** | give protection to |
| **3.** grapple | （　） | **c.** | home to |
| **4.** brunt | （　） | **d.** | reveal |
| **5.** harbor | （　） | **e.** | struggle |

## Summary

次の英文は記事の要約です。下の語群から最も適切な語を１つ選び、（　）内に記入しなさい。

68

Many Koreans think of themselves as a small nation (　　　) to maintain their identity. Hence the rise of (　　　) has made some feel uncomfortable. Islam is often looked at (　　　), so when Muslims established a mosque in the city of Daegu there was local (　　　). But because of labor shortages Korea has little choice but to welcome immigrants and treat them (　　　).

| fairly | hostility | multiculturalism | negatively | struggling |
|---|---|---|---|---|

2022年５月10日に第20代大韓民国大統領に就任した尹錫悦（ユン・ソクヨル）は、1960年12月18日に生まれた。ソウル大卒業後、司法試験を受け続け、９回目で合格して検事になった。「権力から独立した検察」を主張し、朴槿恵（パククネ）元大統領をめぐる贈収賄事件を捜査指揮し、2017年に朴氏を逮捕。文政権に評価され、2019年から2021年まで検察総長を務めた。選挙時の公約として掲げた「大統領府の移転」を踏まえ、当選後に韓国の大統領府の名称を「大統領室」に改名し、移転が正式に決定された。移転後の青瓦台の建物と敷地は公園として国民に開放することになった。また、数え年、実年齢、満年齢の３種類の数え方の統一を、法的・社会的にも満年齢を基準とする法改正を2023年までに進める方針も示した。

　尹錫悦（ユン・ソクヨル）氏の大統領就任後、これまでの文在寅（ムン・ジェイン）政権時代に悪化した日韓関係を革新系から保守系への政権交代で雪解けにつながるのではないかと期待されている。しかし、政治経験のない検察出身の尹氏の手腕は未知数とされ、国会では野党が過半数を占め、政権運営は簡単ではない。日韓の対立が続いているのは、「元慰安婦」と「元徴用工」の問題である。大統領就任式に出席した林芳正外相は「両国間の懸案の本質的な解決に迅速に取り組む必要がある」とする岸田文雄首相の親書を尹氏に渡したが、問題の解決は容易ではない。

## Reading

69

# How 'Multiculturalism' Became a Bad Word in South Korea

DAEGU, South Korea — Inside the dimly lit house, young Muslim men knelt and prayed in silence. Outside, their Korean neighbors gathered with angry signs to protest "a den of terrorists" moving into their neighborhood.

5　　In a densely populated but otherwise quiet district in Daegu, a city in southeastern South Korea, a highly emotional standoff is underway.

Roughly 150 Muslims, mostly students at the nearby Kyungpook National University, started building a mosque
10　in a lot next door to their temporary house of worship about a year ago. When their Korean neighbors found out, they were furious.

The mosque would turn the neighborhood of Daehyeon-dong into "an enclave of Muslims and a crime-infested slum,"
15　the Korean neighbors wrote on signs and protest banners. It would bring more "noise" and a "food smell" from an unfamiliar culture, driving out the Korean residents.

The fault line between the two communities here has exposed an uncomfortable truth in South Korea. At a time
20　when the country enjoys more global influence than ever — with consumers around the world eager to dance to its music, drive its cars and buy its smartphones — it is also grappling with a fierce wave of anti-immigrant fervor and Islamophobia. While it has successfully exported its culture abroad, it has
25　been slow to welcome other cultures at home.

The mosque dispute has become a flash point, part of a larger phenomenon in which South Koreans have had to confront what it means to live in an increasingly diverse society. Muslims have often borne the brunt of racist
30　misgivings, particularly after the Taliban executed two South Korean missionaries in 2007.

Bad Word：悪口、好ましくない言葉

DAEGU：大邱（テグ）《韓国東南部の内陸にある広域市》

signs：プラカード

den：巣窟

standoff：対立

Kyungpook National University：慶北大学

lot：土地、区画

Daehyeon-dong：デヒョン洞

enclave：居留地

fault line：断層線のようなもの、深刻な意見の相違

grappling with ～：～に取り組む、立ち向かう

Islamophobia：イスラム恐怖症

dispute：紛争

confront ～：～に直面する

borne the brunt of ～：～の矢面に立った

misgivings：不安、疑念

Taliban：タリバン《アフガニスタンのイスラム原理主義組織》

executed ～：～を処刑した

missionaries：（キリスト教）宣教師

72

The arrival of 500 Yemeni asylum seekers on the island of Jeju in 2018 triggered South Korea's first series of organized anti-immigrant protests. The government responded to fears
35 that the asylum seekers were harboring terrorists by banning them from leaving the island.

Many Koreans explain their attitude toward foreigners by citing history: their small nation has survived invasions and occupations for centuries, maintaining its territory, language
40 and ethnic identity. Those who oppose the mosque and immigration more broadly have often warned that an influx of foreigners would threaten South Korea's "pure blood" and "ethnic homogeneity."

73

Some say the country does not have much of a choice.

45 South Korea's rise as a cultural powerhouse has coincided with a demographic crisis. Years of low birthrates and rising incomes in urban areas have led to shortages of women who want to marry and live in rural towns. Farms and factories have found it difficult to fill low-wage jobs. Universities lack
50 local students.

To help alleviate the challenges, South Korea opened its doors to workers and students from other nations. Some rural men began to marry foreign women, especially from Vietnam. Yet when the government introduced policies
55 to support "multicultural families," there was a backlash. Suddenly, words like "multiculturalism" and "diversity" became pejorative terms for many South Koreans.

By Choe Sang-Hun
*The New York Times , March 1, 2022*

| | |
|---|---|
| asylum seekers：亡命希望者 | |
| island of Jeju：済州（チェジュ）島 | |
| harboring terrorists：隠れテロリスト | |
| occupations：占領 | |
| ethnic：民族的 | |
| influx：流入 | |
| homogeneity：同質性 | |
| powerhouse：大国 | |
| coincided with ～：～と同時に起きた | |
| demographic：人口動態の | |
| fill jobs：職に就く | |
| local：（地元の）韓国人 | |
| alleviate ～：～を緩和する | |
| backlash：反発 | |
| pejorative：軽蔑的な | |

# Exercises

次の１の英文の質問に答え、２〜５の英文を完成させるために、ａ〜ｄの中から最も適切なものを１つ選びなさい。

1. What does Islamophobia mean?

 **a.** Attraction to the Muslim religion and culture.
 **b.** Fear of the Muslim religion and people.
 **c.** Dislike of Muslim art and architecture.
 **d.** Fondness for Muslim art and ideas.

2. In Daegu, some local Koreans worried that Muslims would create

 **a.** loud noise and strange food smells.
 **b.** poverty and demographic crisis.
 **c.** purity and ethnic homogeneity.
 **d.** consumerism and cultural influence.

3. While exporting its culture to the world, South Korea has

 **a.** warmly embraced other cultures.
 **b.** slowly absorbed migrant cultures.
 **c.** hardly imported foreign cultures.
 **d.** quickly welcomed diverse cultures.

4. The arrival in Jeju of 500 asylum seekers from Yemen

 **a.** triggered terrorist acts in South Korea.
 **b.** helped South Koreans appreciate their global influence.
 **c.** increased support for multiculturalism in South Korea.
 **d.** led South Koreans to start anti-immigrant protests.

5. Koreans' distrust of other cultures could be linked to historical struggles to defend their

 **a.** ethnic identity.
 **b.** cultural popularity.
 **c.** economic expansion.
 **d.** demographic diversity.

本文の内容に合致するものにT（True）、合致しないものにF（False）をつけなさい。

(    ) **1.** Diversity became a negative word for many South Koreans.

(    ) **2.** According to the writer, foreign women come to South Korea's rural areas because of the nation's cultural attractions.

(    ) **3.** Consumers around the world want to dance to South Korea's music and buy its smartphones.

(    ) **4.** It might be said that South Koreans need foreigners, yet do not want them.

(    ) **5.** Many South Koreans seem to associate Muslims with terrorism.

## Vocabulary

次の英文は、読売新聞の The Japan News 「えいご工房」 に掲載された *Yoon elected as new South Korean president*『ユン氏、次期韓国大統領に選出』 の記事の一部です。下の語群から最も適切なものを1つ選び、（   ）内に記入しなさい。

Seoul (AP) — South Korea's President-elect Yoon Sukyeol said on March 10 he would (    ) an alliance with the United States, build up a powerful military and sternly (    ) with North Korean provocations, hours after he won the country's (    ) election to become its next leader.

Yoon, whose single five-year term is to begin in May, said during his campaign he would make a (    ) alliance with the United States the center of his foreign policy. He's accused outgoing liberal President Moon Jae-in of (    ) toward Pyongyang and Beijing and away from Washington. He's also stressed the need to recognize the strategic importance of (    ) ties with Tokyo despite recent bilateral historical disputes.

Some experts say a Yoon government will likely be able to reinforce ties with Washington and improve (    ) with Tokyo but can't really (    ) frictions with Pyongyang and Beijing.

| | | | |
|---|---|---|---|
| avoid | boosted | cope | hard-fought |
| relations | repairing | solidify | tilting |

# ●アフリカでクーデター多発の理由

2020年8月18日、マリのバマにある
独立広場に反乱軍兵士が到着し、住
民たちから歓迎を受ける。その後、
大統領と首相は拘束された

AFP／WAA

## *Before you read*

### Republic of Guinea　ギニア共和国

面積　245,857km²（本州とほぼ同じ）／首都　コナクリ
公用語　フランス語／人口　12,770,000人
宗教　イスラム教、キリスト教／民族　プル、マリンケ
識字率　57%／通貨　ギニア・フラン／政体　共和制
GDP　135.9億ドル／1人当たりのGNI　950ドル

### Burkina Faso　ブルキナ・ファソ

面積　274,200km²（日本の70%）／首都　ワガドゥグ
公用語　フランス語／人口　20,900,000人
宗教　伝統宗教　57%、イスラム教　31%、キリスト教　12%
民族　モシ、グルマンチェ／識字率　57%／通貨　CFAフラン
政体　共和制／GDP　173.7億ドル／1人当たりのGNI　790ドル

### Republic of Chad　チャド共和国

面積　1,284,000km²（日本の3.4倍）／首都　ンジャメナ
公用語　フランス語、アラビア語／民族　サラ、チャド・アラブ
人口　20,250,000人／宗教　イスラム教　52%　キリスト教　44%
識字率　34%／通貨　CFAフラン／政体　共和制
GDP　108.4億ドル／1人当たりのGNI　660ドル

### Republic of Mali　マリ共和国

面積　1,240,000km²（日本の3.3倍）／首都　バマコ
公用語　フランス語／人口　20,250,000人
宗教　イスラム教　80%、キリスト教／民族　バンバラ、プル
識字率　61%／通貨　CFAフラン／政体　共和制
GDP　173.9億ドル／1人当たりのGNI　830ドル

### Republic of Niger　ニジェール共和国

面積　1,267,000km²（日本の3.3倍）／首都　ニアメ
公用語　フランス語／人口　24,210,000人
宗教　イスラム教・スンニ派　90%／民族　ハウサ、ジェルマ
識字率　35%／通貨　CFAフラン／政体　共和制
GDP　136.8億ドル／1人当たりのGNI　540ドル

### The Republic of the Sudan　スーダン共和国

面積　1,880,000km²（日本の約5倍）／首都　ハルツーム
公用語　アラビア語／人口　42,810,000人
宗教　イスラム教、キリスト教／民族　アラブ人、ヌビア人
識字率　69%／通貨　スーダン・ポンド／政体　共和制
GDP　189億ドル／1人当たりのGNI　590ドル

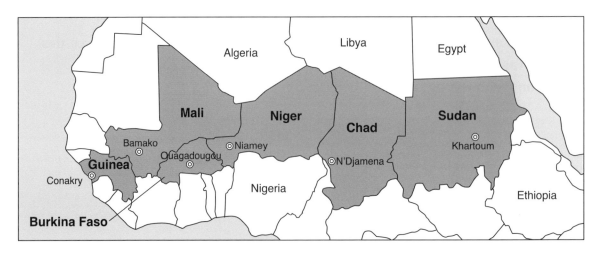

次の1〜5の語句の説明として最も近いものをa〜eから1つ選び、（　）内に記入しなさい。

| | | | | | |
|---|---|---|---|---|---|
| **1.** | ring out | （　） | **a.** | large area | |
| **2.** | dissolve | （　） | **b.** | keep hold of | |
| **3.** | cling to | （　） | **c.** | easily spread | |
| **4.** | contagious | （　） | **d.** | echo | |
| **5.** | swath | （　） | **e.** | close | |

**Summary**

　次の英文は記事の要約です。下の語群から最も適切な語を1つ選び、（　）内に記入しなさい。

　　Military coups (　　　) governments in five African nations in just one and a half years. The (　　　) was in Mali in August, 2020. Then came Chad, (　　　) by Guinea, Sudan and Burkina Faso. There was also an (　　　) coup in Niger. Some people think that if no action is taken against these (　　　) regimes there will be more takeovers in the region.

| attempted | first | followed | illegal | unseated |
|---|---|---|---|---|

　　アフリカのサハラ砂漠南縁部に広がるサヘル地域の情勢悪化が深刻だ。イスラム過激派の「アルカイダ」の関連組織JNIMと「イラク・レバントのイスラム国」のISILが活動を活発化させている。JNIMは、活動地域等をめぐりISILと戦闘を交えている。旧宗主国のフランスは、過激派掃討作戦を続けているが、根絶はかなり難しい。イスラム過激派の台頭は、2011年のリビアのカダフィ政権の崩壊がきっかけとなった。マリに帰国した遊牧民トゥアレグの傭兵の武装蜂起に乗じて過激派が力を蓄え、周辺のブルキナファソ、ニジェールなどの周辺国にも広がった。

　　マリでは、2020年8月以降、2度に渡り軍事クーデターが起きた。22年の1月に、ブルキナファソでは親仏派の大統領に対し反乱軍がクーデターを成功させた。ニジェールでは住民虐殺が止まらず、ナイジェリア、チャド、カメルーンでは「ボコ・ハラム」や「イスラム国」系組織が横行している。サヘルを立て直そうと2013年からフランスは軍事介入を始めたが、土着化したイスラム過激派の力を排除することは困難だ。マリは、ロシアを頼り、プーチン政権に近い民間軍事会社と契約した。サヘルは、地中海沿岸諸国とサハラ以南のアフリカ各国とのつなぎ地域にあたる。混乱をこのままにしておくと、周辺諸国に波及し、欧州への移民や難民が増える恐れがある。

# Reading

## Five African countries. Six coups. Why now?

Gunfire rings out. Rumors spread of a military takeover. The president is nowhere to be seen. The nation turns on the television and collectively switches to the state channel, where they see new leaders, wearing berets and fatigues, announce
5 that the constitution has been suspended, national assembly dissolved, borders closed.

In the past 18 months, in similar scenes, military leaders have toppled the governments of Mali, Chad, Guinea, Sudan and now, Burkina Faso. West African leaders Friday called
10 an emergency summit on the situation in Burkina Faso, at which the new military leader, Lt. Col. Paul-Henri Damiba, told the nation in his first public address Thursday night that he would return the country to constitutional order "when the conditions are right."

15 The resurgence of coups has alarmed the region's remaining civilian leaders. Ghana's president, Nana Akufo-Addo, said Friday, "It represents a threat to peace, security and stability in West-Africa."

These five nations that have recently experienced military
20 coups form a broken line that stretches across the wide bulge of Africa, from Guinea on the west coast to Sudan in the east.

First came Mali, in August 2020. The military took advantage of public anger at a stolen parliamentary election and the government's failure to protect its people from violent
25 extremists, and arrested President Ibrahim Boubacar Keita and forced him to resign on state television. Mali actually had two coups in a nine-month span.

An unusual coup unfolded in Chad in April 2021. A president who had ruled for three decades was killed on the
30 battlefield, and his son was quickly installed in his place — a violation of the constitution.

In March 2021, there was a failed coup attempt in Niger,

| | |
|---|---|
| coups：クーデター、政変 | |
| takeover：乗っ取り、権力奪取 | |
| berets：ベレー帽 | |
| fatigues：戦闘服 | |
| constitution：憲法 | |
| suspended：停止された | |
| national assembly：国会 | |
| dissolved：解散された | |
| called ～：～を召集した | |
| Lt. Col.：中佐 | |
| public address：国民に向けた演説 | |
| "when the conditions are right"：「条件が整えば」 | |
| resurgence：再流行 | |
| broken line：破線 | |
| bulge：膨らみ | |
| took advantage of ～：～を利用した | |
| parliamentary：議会の | |
| extremists：過激派 | |
| resign：辞任する | |
| unfolded：起きた | |
| installed in ～：～に任命された | |

then in September 2021, it was Guinea's turn: A high-ranking officer trained by the United States overthrew a president who had tried to cling to power. Then in October, it was Sudan's: The country's top generals seized power, tearing up a power-sharing deal that was supposed to lead to the country's first free election in decades.

That's more than 114 million people now ruled by soldiers who have illegally seized power. There were four successful coups in Africa in 2021 — there hadn't been that many in a single calendar year since 1999. United Nations Secretary-General Antonio Guterres called it "an epidemic of coup d'etats."

Coups are contagious. When the Malian government fell, analysts warned that Burkina Faso could follow. Now that it has, they're warning that if the coup plotters aren't punished, there will be more coups in the region.

People are fed up with their governments for many reasons — major security threats, relentless humanitarian disasters and millions of young people having no prospects.

Governments are performing abysmally, said Abdul Zanya Salifu, a scholar at the University of Calgary in Alberta, Canada, who focuses on the Sahel, the swath of Africa that lies just below the Sahara. So, he said, the military thinks: "You know, why not take over?"

By Ruth Maclean
*The New York Times, January 31, 2022*

generals：将軍

seized power：権力を掌握した

tearing up 〜：〜を破棄する

power-sharing deal：権限分割協定

Secretary-General：事務総長

epidemic：流行

contagious：伝染する

plotters：首謀者

fed up with 〜：〜にうんざりしている

humanitarian：人道的

prospects：将来の見通し

Sahel：サヘル《サハラ砂漠南縁にある地域》

swath：帯状の土地

# Exercises

次の1～5の英文を完成させるために、a～dの中から最も適切なものを1つ選びなさい。

1. The governments of Mali, Chad, Guinea, Sudan and Burkina Faso

    **a.** were recently overthrown by military leaders.

    **b.** have launched military attacks on neighboring countries.

    **c.** have recently experienced failed coups.

    **d.** are clinging to power despite attempted coups.

2. Nana Akufo-Addo believes the military takeovers

    **a.** represent constitutional order.

    **b.** indicate peaceful political transition.

    **c.** threaten African stability.

    **d.** resulted in African security.

3. In April 2021, the president who had ruled Chad for thirty years

    **a.** was arrested.

    **b.** was killed.

    **c.** launched a coup.

    **d.** put his son in power.

4. The UN Secretary-General

    **a.** warned Africans that they would get ill.

    **b.** said the coups would never stop.

    **c.** criticized Africa's health policies.

    **d.** compared the events to a disease.

5. Many young Africans are sick of governments that seem to offer them

    **a.** successive takeovers.

    **b.** hope for change.

    **c.** no future.

    **d.** military power.

本文の内容に合致するものにＴ（True)、合致しないものにＦ（False）をつけなさい。

( 　 ) **1.** The military coups began in the north of Africa and ended in the south.

( 　 ) **2.** The first in this string of coups occurred in Mali.

( 　 ) **3.** In Guinea, an American-trained officer overthrew the president.

( 　 ) **4.** Over the last two decades Africa has experienced about four coups every year.

( 　 ) **5.** Abdul Zanya Salifu says African military figures often feel they can perform better than civilian leaders.

**Vocabulary**

次の１〜8は、アフリカのサヘル諸国に関する英文です。下記の国名から１つ選び（ 　 ）内に、そして、地図からａ〜ｈを選び［ 　 ］内に記入しなさい。

**1.** ( 　 　 　 ) has borders with Libya, Niger, Nigeria, Cameroon, Central African Republic and Sudan, and its capital is Ndjamena. [ 　 ]

**2.** ( 　 　 　 ) is a country in eastern Africa and its capital is Khartoum. [ 　 ]

**3.** ( 　 　 　 )'s capital is Bamako and its main language is French. [ 　 ]

**4.** ( 　 　 　 ) is a small country and has borders with Djibouti, Ethiopia and Sudan. [ 　 ]

**5.** ( 　 　 　 ) is a large republic in western Africa facing the Gulf of Guinea. [ 　 ]

**6.** ( 　 　 　 )'s currency is called the Guinean franc. [ 　 ]

**7.** ( 　 　 　 ) is a country south of Mali and its capital is Ouagadougou. [ 　 ]

**8.** ( 　 　 　 ) has borders with Libya, Algeria, Mali, Burkina Faso, Benin, Nigeria and Chad. [ 　 ]

| Burkina Faso | Chad | Eritrea | Guinea |
| Mali | Niger | Nigeria | Sudan |

## ●リオのカーニバルのパレードを巡り争い騒ぎ

ブラジルのリオデジャネイロ市当局がストリート系サンバチーム「ブロコス」のカーニバル参加を禁止すると、2022年4月13日、それに抗議して、街中でサンバを踊る市民たち　　　　　　　　　　　　　　　　　　　　AP／アフロ

## *Before you read*

### Federative Republic of Brazil
### ブラジル連邦共和国

面積　8,512,000km²（日本の22.5倍）（世界５位）
人口　209,470,000人（世界６位）
民族　ヨーロッパ系　48%、アフリカ系　８％
　　　アジア系　1.1%、混血　43%
　　　先住民　0.4%
首都　ブラジリア
最大都市　サンパウロ
公用語　ポルトガル語
宗教　キリスト教・カトリック　65%
　　　キリスト教・プロテスタント　22%
　　　無宗教　８％
GDP　１兆8,850億米ドル
　　　１人当たりのGNI　9,080米ドル
通貨　レアル
政体　連邦共和制
識字率　93.2%

次の1〜5の語句の説明として最も近いものをa〜eから1つ選び、（　　）内に記入しなさい。

1. riotous　　　　　（　　）
2. shindig　　　　　（　　）
3. glitter-smeared　（　　）
4. plead for　　　　（　　）
5. brandish　　　　　（　　）

a. party
b. carry
c. demand or ask desperately
d. covered in decorations
e. chaotic and noisy

**Summary**

　次の英文は記事の要約です。下の語群から最も適切な語を1つ選び、（　　）内に記入しなさい。

80

　After being (　　　) for two years, Rio's carnival will take place in the Sambódromo stadium. Some private events will also be (　　　). But the colorful street parades have not been (　　　) permission to return as the city authorities claim there has been insufficient time to prepare. In addition to being (　　　), many local groups feel (　　　) against.

| allowed | cancelled | disappointed | discriminated | given |

　リオデジャネイロのカーニバル（Carnaval do Rio de Janeiro）は、復活祭前の40日間に及ぶ四旬節の期間に入る前に行われる世界最大規模の祭りである。パレードとサンバ、打楽器の演奏が結び付いたカーニバルは、「地上最大のショー」とも言われている。その歴史は、1723年にまで遡る。ダンスは、かつて奴隷たちがアフリカからもたらされ、都市の外縁部の貧しい集落で人気のあるサンバである。バトゥカーダという、主に打楽器演奏を基盤にした音楽で、リオのカーニバルにはなくてはならないものである。この音楽は、「歌いながら、踊りながら、パレードすることを可能にするようなリズムが必要とされて、誕生したものである」。パレードは賞金付きコンテスト形式になっており審査が行われる。観客席が設けられ、約6万人のダンサーを約150万人の観客が見る。
　「リオのカーニバル」は、ブラジルのリオデジャネイロで毎年夏に開かれるが、2021年は新型コロナウイルスの影響で史上初めて中止となり、今年2022年もオミクロン株の感染拡大で、当初2月下旬に予定されていた開催が、2か月延期された。およそ2年ぶりの開催となったカーニバルは、4月22日夜、12のグルーポ・エスペシャル・チームが歌やダンスの美しさなどを披露した。熱気が最高潮を迎えた。それぞれのチームは2500人から最大3600人のメンバーで構成され、華麗な衣装を身につけたダンサーたちが、大がかりな山車とともに、特別会場に設けられた700メートルの花道を行進した。中央の打楽器隊だけでも200人から250人で編成されている。コンテストは、名門 Grande Rio が優勝、Beija Flor が準優勝を飾った。ブラジルでは、新型コロナウイルスに感染して68万人が亡くなっている。

# Reading

81

## Rio carnival groups fight for right to party ahead of official celebrations

Rio's world-famous samba schools will return to action next week for their first parades at the Sambódromo stadium in more than two years. But the carnival enthusiasts behind hundreds of "*blocos*" — riotous musical troupes that roam the
5 streets clutching brass instruments and booze — are furious they have not received authorization to gather.

82

The Omicron variant scuppered plans for this year's pre-Lenten carnival, which should have been held in late February. But while the Sambódromo competition was rearranged for
10 next weekend — and often expensive private shindigs are also taking place — authorities claim there was insufficient time to prepare for the free outdoor blocos, which attract hundreds of thousands of partygoers.

More than 120 blocos denounced their sidelining this
15 week in a manifesto that declared: "The streets belong to the people and we are free to speak."

Hundreds of glitter-smeared carnival activists pranced through downtown Rio on Wednesday night to protest what they called a hammer-blow to the local economy and one of
20 Brazil's most important cultural treasures.

83

"The city hall has abandoned street carnival," complained Kiko Horta, a founder of one of Rio's best-known blocos, the Cordão do Boitatá.

"It makes no sense. Street carnival — along with the
25 [Sambódromo] carnival — is the city's most important festival. It has tremendous symbolic, cultural and economic value. Simply forbidding it is absurd," Horta added.

Telma Neves, the president of the samba bloco Engata no Centro (City Centre Coupling), joined the demo with her
30 83-year-old mother Georgina who had not missed a carnival since she was six. "We've spent the last two years in silence,

---

Rio：リオデジャネイロ《ブラジルの都市》

carnival：カーニバル、謝肉祭《カトリック国で四旬節（Lent）の断食に入る直前に行われる祭り》

party：どんちゃん騒ぎをする

first ~ in more than two years：2年ぶりの~

"*blocos*"：「ブロコス」《ストリートカーニバル・グループ》

troupes：一座、一行

brass instruments：金管楽器

booze：酒

authorization：許可

Omicron variant：オミクロン変異株《新型コロナウイルスの変異株》

pre-Lenten：四旬節前の

shindigs：大騒ぎ

sidelining：傍観者にされたこと

glitter-smeared：キラキラに染まった

pranced through ~：~を跳ね回った

Cordão do Boitatá：ボイタタ（火蛇）グループ

absurd：馬鹿げてる

Engata no Centro：エンガタ・ノ・セントロ《都心連合（結）》

missed ~：~を休んだ

unable to do anything," Neves, 58, complained. "We're pleading for the right to our own carnival."

35 Wednesday's rally offered a snapshot of the weird and wonderful world of Rio street carnival, as bacchanals of all ages and from all walks of life danced through town wearing a dizzying medley of costumes — or in some cases almost no clothes at all.

One man came dressed as a grim reaper brandishing a 40 Minion toy and a pretend syringe — a political critique of President Jair Bolsonaro's denialist response to Covid.

Claudio Manhães, a 43-year-old x-ray technician, came to represent his group — founded by a gang of samba-loving radiology professionals and called Te Vejo Por Dentro, or I 45 Can See Your Insides. "We thought this year's carnival would be a super carnival like in 1919 after the Spanish flu," Manhães said, showing off photographs of the green T-shirts his bloco had printed for a party that would no longer take place.

"It's sad. There were so many expectations," Manhães 50 sighed.

Tarcísio Motta, a leftist councillor who has criticised the government's treatment of the blocos, questioned whether Rio's mayor wanted to cast himself as "an enemy of carnival". "The city hall is right to support the samba schools ... but why 55 haven't they done the same for street carnival?" Motta asked, accusing authorities of depriving residents of their legal right to carnival.

By Tom Phillips
*The Guardian News & Media Ltd, April 14, 2022*

---

rally：集会

bacchanals：どんちゃん騒ぎをする人《バッカス神が語源》

all walks of life：あらゆる職業や地位の人々

grim reaper：死神

Minion：ミニオン《映画キャラクター；最強最悪の人物に使える（この場合は大統領が死神を暗示)》

denialist：否認主義者の

Covid：コロナウイルス感染症

radiology professionals：放射線学専門家

Spanish flu：スペイン風邪《世界で2,000万人から4,000万人が死亡したとされる》

showing off 〜：〜を見せびらかす

expectations：期待

councillor：議員

accusing 〜 of …：〜が…したと非難する

depriving 〜 of …：〜から…を奪う

# Exercises

**Multiple Choice**

次の１～５の英文を完成させるために、a～dの中から最も適切なものを１つ選びなさい。

1. _____, but street activists and enthusiasts haven't received permission to get together.

    **a.** Rio's tango groups will be able to return to action
    **b.** Rio's samba schools will return to action
    **c.** Rio's "blocos" have been invited to parade
    **d.** Rio's carnival will be just how it was before the pandemic

2. Plans for the pre-Lenten carnival in late February, 2022,

    **a.** were postponed until the following weekend.
    **b.** were implemented despite the pandemic.
    **c.** were discontinued because of the Omicron variant.
    **d.** were halted by a flu outbreak.

3. Rio's street carnival has been

    **a.** of economic as well as cultural significance.
    **b.** forbidden for many years.
    **c.** held inside a stadium for the last two years.
    **d.** of little interest to Brazilians for a long time.

4. Telma Neves' mother Georgina _____ since she was six.

    **a.** had not joined a carnival
    **b.** had not missed a carnival
    **c.** had not experienced a carnival
    **d.** had not prohibited a carnival

5. Claudio Manhães had hoped this year's carnival would be

    **a.** an extraordinary one like in 1919 after Covid-19.
    **b.** an exceptional one like in 2008 after the financial crisis.
    **c.** a superb one like in 1991 after the influenza outbreak.
    **d.** a super one like in 1919 after the Spanish flu.

本文の内容に合致するものにT（True）、合致しないものにF（False）をつけなさい。

(    ) **1.** The city hall in Rio de Janeiro gave its support to street carnival.

(    ) **2.** Carnival enthusiasts have spent the last two years performing.

(    ) **3.** Carnival participants usually dance to brass bands on the streets.

(    ) **4.** Street carnival in Brazil has symbolic, cultural and economic value.

(    ) **5.** Telma Neves is president of the samba bloco Te Vejo Por Dentro.

## Vocabulary

次の（1）～（6）はキリスト教のカトリックの年中行事です。該当する英語説明文を下のa～fの中から1つ選び（　）内に、そして行事を時系列に並べ、[　]内に2～6までの順番を入れなさい。

| | | |
|---|---|---|
| **(1)** Ash Wednesday | (    ) | [      ] |
| **(2)** Carnival | (    ) | [   1   ] |
| **(3)** Christmas | (    ) | [      ] |
| **(4)** Easter | (    ) | [      ] |
| **(5)** Lent | (    ) | [      ] |
| **(6)** Mardi Gras | (    ) | [      ] |

**a.** a Christian holy day in March or April when Christians remember the death of Christ and his return to life

**b.** the day before the first day of Lent

**c.** the day when Christians celebrate the birth of Christ

**d.** the 40 days before Easter, during which Christians customarily eat less food

**e.** the first day of Lent, when some Christians put ashes on their foreheads as a sign of Penitence

**f.** public dancing, eating, drinking, processions and shows held in Roman Catholic countries in the weeks before Lent

# Unit **15**

## ● ビゴレクシア（筋肉醜形恐怖症）とは

プロテインを持つボディビルダー。若い男性の憧れ？　　　　アフロ

## *Before you read*

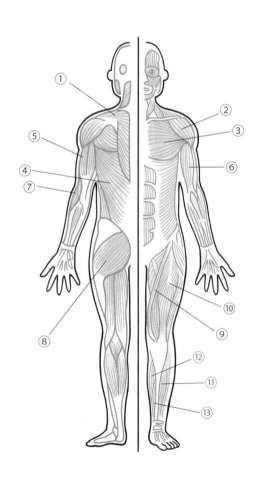

| | | |
|---|---|---|
| **a.** | Biceps （上腕二頭筋） | [　　] |
| **b.** | Brachioradialis （腕とう骨筋） | [　　] |
| **c.** | Deltoid （三角筋） | [　　] |
| **d.** | Gastrocnemius （ひふく筋） | [　　] |
| **e.** | Gluteus maximus （大殿筋） | [　　] |
| **f.** | Latissimus dorsi （広背筋） | [　　] |
| **g.** | Pectoralis major （大胸筋） | [　　] |
| **h.** | Rectus （大腿直筋） | [　　] |
| **i.** | Sartorius （縫工筋） | [　　] |
| **j.** | Soleus （ひらめ筋） | [　　] |
| **k.** | Tibialis anterior （前脛骨筋） | [　　] |
| **l.** | Trapezius （僧帽筋） | [　　] |
| **m.** | Triceps brachii （上腕三頭筋） | [　　] |

**86**　Unit 15

次の1〜5の語句の説明として最も近いものをa〜eから1つ選び、（　）内に記入しなさい。

1. whip into shape     （　）    a. impossible to reach
2. fall behind on      （　）    b. full of muscles
3. unattainable       （　）    c. train and improve
4. beefcake-saturated   （　）    d. fail to keep up with
5. mesomorphic       （　）    e. compact and muscular

**Summary**

次の英文は記事の要約です。下の語群から最も適切な語を1つ選び、（　）内に記入しなさい。

86

Research shows that young women can be harmed by social media's
(　　　) with body image. However, young men may become (　　　) too.
One 16-year-old spends almost as much time (　　　) images of himself on
TikTok as he does (　　　) out. With 400,000 followers he seems happy, but
other boys might experience anxiety when (　　　) themselves with him.

comparing     obsessed     obsession     posting     working

    ビゴレクシア（Bigorexia）は、身体が小さすぎる、または筋肉が不足しているという考えに執着する筋肉醜形恐怖症として定義されている。外観への執着、ミラーチェック、食事と栄養補助食品の固定、関連する薬物療法とステロイドの使用、気分の落ち込みや怒りにつながる外見への不満が特徴だと言われている。筋肉隆々としているのに、何時間も鏡の前に立ち、体のあらゆる部分を調べ、筋肉量を欠いている細い男しか見えない。同じことが拒食症の女性にも当てはまる。鏡を見ると、骸骨のように痩身なのに、まだ太っていると思っている。この病気の主な原因は、その外観に対する不満の高まりで、治療を必要とする精神障害である。

    ステロイドの定期的な使用は中毒性があるため、悪循環から抜け出すことは困難だ。サプリメント（ステロイドまたはホルモン）を使用すると、肝臓がんや肺がんを含む多くの病気の発症を引き起こす。その結果、前立腺肥大または女性化乳房と精子の質の低下が起こる。腎臓や肝臓に永久的な損傷を与えるものもあり、動脈硬化症の変化を増加させるため、心臓発作や脳卒中が頻繁に起こる。神経性食欲不振症も身体醜形障害の一種だ。ジムで何時間も過ごしたり、体の限界をはるかに超えて押したり、戻ってやり直さなければならないと感じたりする。翌日体重を減らし、終わらない筋肉を追加するための食事療法に従う。自分の体を嫌い、身体部分を欠点のように感じる。治療せずに放置すると、強迫性障害が悪化し、ステロイドの誤用やうつ病を引き起こす可能性がある。

# Reading

87

## What Is 'Bigorexia'?

Like many high school athletes, Bobby, 16, a junior from Long Island, has spent years whipping his body into shape through protein diets and workouts.

Between rounds of Fortnite and homework, Bobby goes
5 online to study bodybuilders like Greg Doucette, a 46-year-old fitness personality who has more than 1.3 million YouTube subscribers. Bobby also hits his local gym as frequently as six days a week.

88

He makes sure to hit the fridge, too, grazing on protein-
10 packed Kodiak Cakes and muscle-mass-building Oreo shakes. He consumes so much protein that classmates sometimes gawk at him for eating upward of eight chicken-and-rice meals at school.

But Bobby isn't getting buff so he can stand out during
15 varsity tryouts. His goal is to compete in a different arena: TikTok.

Bobby now posts his own workout TikToks. Shot on his iPhone 11, usually at the gym or in his family's living room, the videos are devoted to topics like how to get a "gorilla
20 chest," "Popeye forearms" or "Lil Uzi's abs."

Bobby said that he has occasionally fallen behind on his schoolwork because he dedicates so much time to weight lifting and prepping high-protein meals.

89

"When Bobby first started posting his videos, our family
25 did not even know what he was doing for months, as he was extremely independent and did stuff on his own," said his father, 49, who is a correctional officer at Rikers Island.

Bobby's father can, in some ways, relate. "When I was younger, I remember seeing the men's fashion magazines and
30 seeing the jacked, buff guys on there and wanted to look like them," he said. "It took me a while to realize that those men's bodies were most likely unattainable."

'Bigorexia'：「ビゴレクシア（筋肉醜形恐怖症）」《自分の体が実際にはたくましいのに貧弱ではないかと慢性的に不安に思ってしまう精神障害》

Long Island：ロング・アイランド《ニューヨーク都市圏に含まれる島》

whipping ～ into shape：～を鍛えて希望通りの形に仕上げる

Fortnite：フォートナイト《バトルロワイアル形式のオンラインゲーム》

personality：有名人

subscribers：加入者

hits ～：～に立ち寄る

Kodiak Cakes：コディアック・ケーキ《パンケーキ製造会社》

Oreo shakes：オレオのミルクセーキ《オレオはクッキーで有名》

upward of ～：～を超える

getting buff：マッチョになる

varsity tryouts：高校代表チーム選手選抜試験

devoted to ～：～をテーマにしている

"Lil Uzi's abs"：「リル・ウージーの腹筋」《大富豪のラッパー》

did stuff：何でもした

correctional officer：刑務官、看守

Rikers Island：ライカーズ島《ニューヨーク市内イースト・リバーの中洲の島で州の主要な刑務所がある》

relate：理解する

jacked：非常に良く発達した筋肉を持った

90

But unlike his father's experience, as Bobby's body mass grows, so does his online audience. "Young guys see me as their idol," said Bobby, who has more than 400,000 followers on TikTok. "They want to be just like me, someone who gained muscle as a teenager."

For many boys and young men, muscle worship has become practically a digital rite of passage in today's beefcake-saturated culture. Examples are everywhere — the hypermasculine video games they play, the mesomorphic superheroes in the movies they watch. The top grossing films of last year were ruled by C.G.I.-enhanced masculine clichés: Spider-Man, Shang Chi, Venom and the entire Marvel universe.

91

Many doctors and researchers say that the relentless online adulation of muscular male bodies can have a toxic effect on the self-esteem of young men, with the never-ending scroll of six packs and boy-band faces making them feel inadequate and anxious.

And while there has been increased public awareness about how social media can be harmful to teenagers — spurred in part by the leak of internal research from Facebook showing that the company hid the negative effects of Instagram — much of that focus has been on girls.

Recent reports, however, have found that those same online pressures can also cause teenage boys to feel bad about their bodies.

By Alex Hawgood
*The New York Times, March 5, 2022*

---

body mass：体重

someone：《同格なので前に「つまり」を置く》

rite of passage：通過儀礼

beefcake：男性肉体美

〜 -saturated：〜で飽和した、溢れかえった

hypermasculine：超男性的な

mesomorphic：頑丈な筋肉のがっしりした体質を持つ

top grossing：最高の興行収益を上げた

C.G.I.：コンピュータ生成画像

clichés：定型

Marvel universe：《アメリカン・コミックの老舗出版社マーベル・コミックス社の作品を映画化した世界》

adulation：誇大な賞賛

self-esteem：自尊心

six packs：シックス・パック《鍛えられた腹筋によって六つに分かれて見える腹部》

boy-band：男性アイドルグループの

feel inadequate：無力だと感じる

feel bad：不快感を覚える

# *Exercises*

次の１〜２の英文の質問に答え、３〜５の英文を完成させるために、 ａ〜ｄの中から最も適切なものを１つ選びなさい。

1. What is 'Bigorexia'?

   **a.** A health condition causing someone to think constantly about muscle.

   **b.** A mental condition causing someone continually to be on a diet.

   **c.** A physical condition making people obsessed with gymnastics.

   **d.** A spiritual condition making people want to stay in good health.

2. What is beefcake-saturated culture?

   **a.** A diet based on the consumption of beef.

   **b.** A lifestyle centered on muscle-appreciation.

   **c.** An interest in cooking and baking.

   **d.** An obsession with superheroes in the movies.

3. Bobby has been training to

   **a.** remain slim through protein diets and workouts.

   **b.** become strong by reducing his food intake.

   **c.** build his body through protein diets and workouts.

   **d.** increase his body mass by only drinking shakes.

4. Many doctors say that the online admiration of muscular males

   **a.** can lead young men to try detoxification diets.

   **b.** can have a toxic effect on young men's self-worth.

   **c.** can lead to toxic waste in boys' bodies.

   **d.** can make boys treat each other toxically.

5. The online pressures can make boys

   **a.** feel good about their bodies.

   **b.** get tired of the hours they spend at the gym.

   **c.** become bored with their bodies.

   **d.** grow anxious about their physical appearance.

本文の内容に合致するものにＴ（True）、合致しないものにＦ（False）をつけなさい。

（　　）**1.** Bobby spends hours at the gym every single day.

（　　）**2.** Bobby has sometimes failed to keep up with his schoolwork.

（　　）**3.** Many boys and young men watch the strong masculine superheroes in the movies.

（　　）**4.** When Bobby's father was young, he too would hit his local gym.

（　　）**5.** Fitness personality Greg Doucette has over 1.5 million YouTube subscribers.

**Vocabulary**

次の１〜８は、「筋トレ」に関する英文です。日本文に合わせて、適切な語を下の語群から１つ選び、（　　）内に記入しなさい。

**1.** １週間に４回ジムに通って、筋トレしている。
I go to the gym and (　　　　) four times a week.

**2.** 引き締まった身体だね。
You have a (　　　　) body.

**3.** ジムに入りびたっていた。
I was one of the gym (　　　　).

**4.** 上腕二頭筋を鍛えるため、ダンベル運動をやっている。
I've been doing dumbbell exercises to strengthen my (　　　　).

**5.** 腹筋見て！６つに割れたよ！
Look at my (　　　　) muscles! I got a six-pack!

**6.** 帰宅後、毎日腕立て伏せをやっている。
I do (　　　　) every day after I get home.

**7.** 腹筋よりストレッチの方が好きだ。
I prefer stretching rather than (　　　　).

**8.** 体脂肪率を下げるのに一番良い方法は何ですか？
What is the most efficient way to get (　　　　)?

| abdominal | biceps | push-ups | rats |
|-----------|--------|----------|------|
| shredded  | sit-ups | toned   | work out |

**15章版：ニュースメディアの英語**

──演習と解説2023年度版──

検印
省略

©2023年1月31日　初 版 発 行

| 編著者 | 高橋　優身 |
| | 伊藤　典子 |
| | Richard Powell |
| 発行者 | 小川　洋一郎 |
| 発行所 | 株式会社朝日出版社 |

101-0065　東京都千代田区西神田3-3-5
電話（03）3239-0271
FAX（03）3239-0479
e-mail: text-e@asahipress.com
振替口座　00140-2-46008
組版・製版／信毎書籍印刷株式会社